First Grade

Everyday Mathematics®

Math Masters

First Grade

Everyday Mathematics®

Math Masters

The University of Chicago
School Mathematics Project

 Wright Group

The McGraw·Hill Companies

Horizontal Number Grid

0									1
10	9	8	7	6	5	4	3	2	11
20	19	18	17	16	15	14	13	12	21
30	29	28	27	26	25	24	23	22	31
40	39	38	37	36	35	34	33	32	41
50	49	48	47	46	45	44	43	42	51
60	59	58	57	56	55	54	53	52	61
70	69	68	67	66	65	64	63	62	71
80	79	78	77	76	75	74	73	72	81
90	89	88	87	86	85	84	83	82	91
100	99	98	97	96	95	94	93	92	101
110	109	108	107	106	105	104	103	102	101

Use with Lesson 2.1.

Make a Number Line

Cut out each row. Glue or tape the rows together to make a number line.

41	31	21	11	1	9
42	32	22	12	2	8
43	33	23	13	3	7
44	34	24	14	4	6
45	35	25	15	5	5
46	36	26	16	6	4
47	37	27	17	7	3
48	38	28	18	8	2
49	39	29	19	9	1
50	40	30	20	10	0
↓	Glue	Glue	Glue	Glue	Glue

Use with Lesson 2.1.

Hands

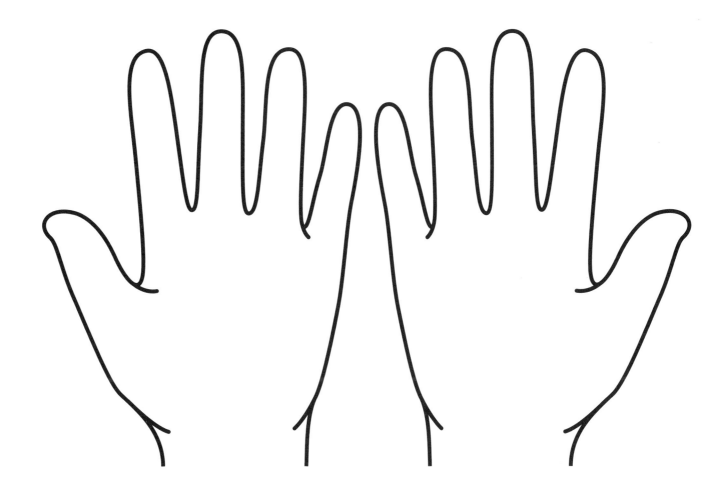

Use with Lesson 2.3.

Combinations for _____ Pennies

Name _____

Name _____

Combinations for _____ Pennies

Unit
pennies

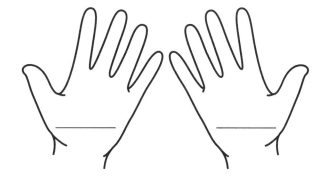

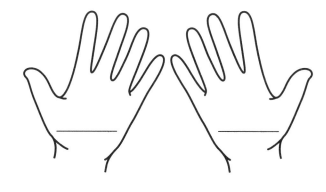

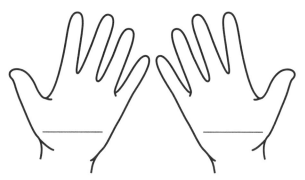

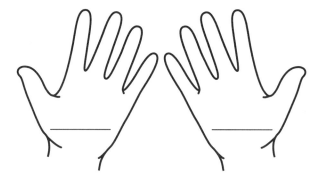

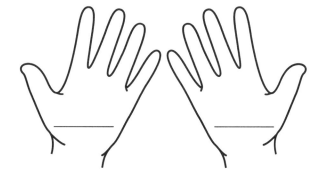

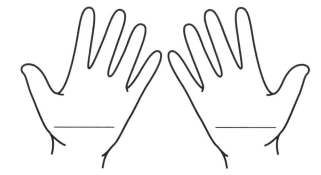

               Use with Lesson 2.4.

Paper Clock with Hour Hand

1. Cut out the clock face and the hour hand.

2. Punch a hole through the center of the clock face. Punch a hole through the X on the hour hand.

3. Fasten the hand to the clock face with a brad.

hour hand

a brad

Clock Faces

_____

_____

_____

_____

Paper Clock

1. Fill in the missing numbers.

2. Cut out the clock face. Then cut out the hands.

3. Punch a hole through the center of the clock face. Then punch holes through the X's on the hands.

4. Place the hour hand on top of the minute hand. Then fasten both hands to the clock face with a brad.

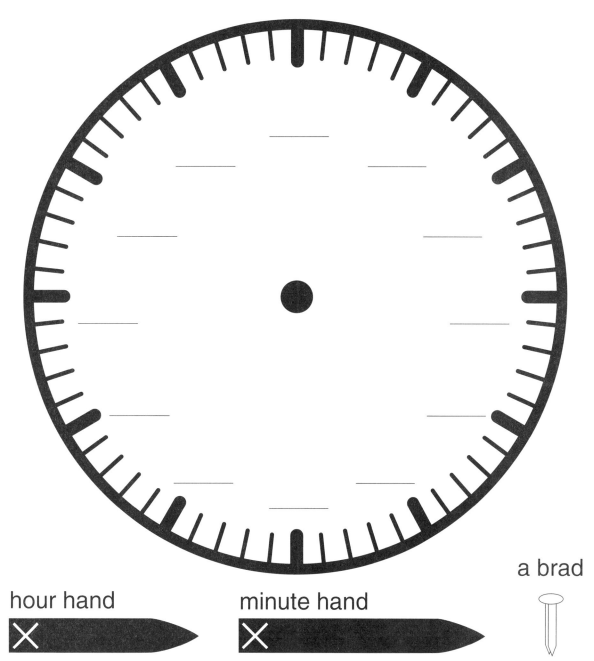

a brad

hour hand   minute hand

More Clock Faces

1.

_____ o'clock

2.

_____ o'clock

3.

_____ o'clock

4.

_____ o'clock

5.

_____ o'clock

6.

_____ o'clock

Use with Lesson 2.6.

How Long Is It?

Materials ❑ ruler

❑ about 8 objects

1. Look at your ruler.

Try to remember how long it is.

Then put it away in your tool kit.

2. Put the objects you think are longer than your ruler into one pile.

Put the objects you think are shorter than your ruler into another pile.

3. Take out your ruler and check your guesses.

4. Now, put the objects in order from shortest to longest.

Show your objects to your teacher.

Counting by 2s

Count by 2s to connect the dots. Use your ruler.

Then color your finished design.

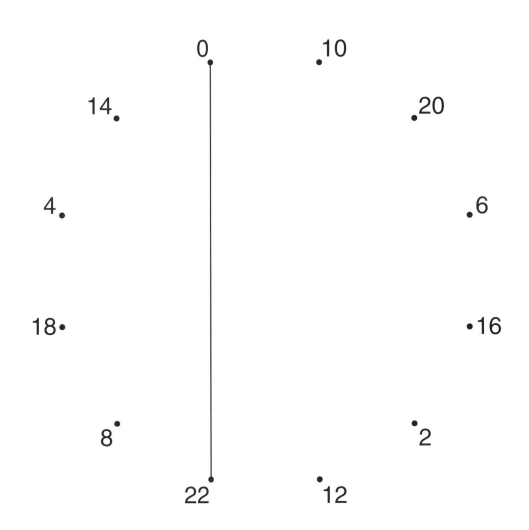

Sorting Dominoes

Materials ☐ 2 sets of dominoes

1. Put all dominoes with a blank half in a pile. Then sort them into matching pairs.

2. Put all dominoes that show 1 dot in a pile. Sort them into matching pairs.

3. Put all dominoes that show 2 dots in a pile. Sort them into matching pairs.

4. Put all dominoes that show 3 dots in a pile. Sort them into matching pairs.

5. Continue until all dominoes are sorted into matching pairs.

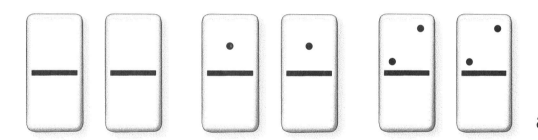 and so on.

Show your matching pairs to your teacher.

Then sort the dominoes back into two sets of dominoes.

Nickel/Penny Grab Record Sheet

1. Grab a handful of coins. Guess how much money you grabbed. Record your guess.

I guess my total is _____ cents.

2. Count the coins.

I have _____ nickels. I have _____ pennies.

That's _____ cents in all.

3. Trade your nickels for pennies.

Now I have _____ pennies.

Use with Lesson 2.14.

- -

Nickel/Penny Grab Record Sheet

1. Grab a handful of coins. Guess how much money you grabbed. Record your guess.

I guess my total is _____ cents.

2. Count the coins.

I have _____ nickels. I have _____ pennies.

That's _____ cents in all.

3. Trade your nickels for pennies.

Now I have _____ pennies.

     Use with Lesson 2.14.

Before and After

Materials   ☐ cards 0–10 (4 of each number)

Players   2

Directions

1. Mix the cards.

2. Deal 6 cards to each player.

3. Put 2 cards down side by side and faceup.

4. Put the rest of the cards facedown in a stack.

5. Take turns. When it is your turn:

- Look for any number in your hand that comes *before* or *after* one of the faceup numbers. Put it on top of the faceup number. Play as many cards as you can.

- Take as many cards as you need from the stack so that you have 6 cards again.

- If you can't play any cards when it is your turn, take 2 cards from the stack. Place them faceup on top of the 2 faceup cards. Try to play cards from your hand again. If you still can't, your turn is over.

6. The game is over when:

- There are no more cards left in the stack

- No one can play any more cards.

7. The player holding fewer cards at the end wins.

Diamonds

     Use with Lesson 3.1.

Name _____   Date _____

									0
1	2	3	4	5	6	7	8	9	10
11	12	13	14	15	16	17	18	19	20
21	22	23	24	25	26	27	28	29	30
31	32	33	34	35	36	37	38	39	40
41	42	43	44	45	46	47	48	49	50
51	52	53	54	55	56	57	58	59	60
61	62	63	64	65	66	67	68	69	70
71	72	73	74	75	76	77	78	79	80
81	82	83	84	85	86	87	88	89	90
91	92	93	94	95	96	97	98	99	100
101	102	103	104	105	106	107	108	109	110
111	112	113	114	115	116	117	118	119	120

Use with Lesson 3.3.

Number Sequences

									0
1	2	3	4	5	6	7	8	9	10
11	12	13	14	15	16	17	18	19	20
21	22	23	24	25	26	27	28	29	30
31	32	33	34	35	36	37	38	39	40
41	42	43	44	45	46	47	48	49	50
51	52	53	54	55	56	57	58	59	60
61	62	63	64	65	66	67	68	69	70
71	72	73	74	75	76	77	78	79	80
81	82	83	84	85	86	87	88	89	90
91	92	93	94	95	96	97	98	99	100
101	102	103	104	105	106	107	108	109	110

Color the following numbers on the number grid.

Fill in the rest of the numbers below. Use the grid to help you.

Circle the ones digit in each 2-digit number.

___2___, ___5___, ___8___, _____, __14__, _____, _____,

__23__, _____, _____, __32__, _____, _____, _____,

__44__, _____, _____, __53__, _____, _____, _____

Use with Lesson 3.3.

Domino Sort

Materials ☐ 1 set of dominoes

☐ *Math Masters*, page 24

1. Work in a group of four.

- One person finds all the dominoes with an even number of dots on both sides.

- Another person finds all the dominoes with an odd number of dots on both sides.

- The other two people find all the dominoes with an odd number of dots on one side and an even number of dots on the other side.

2. Record the dominoes in your pile on page 24. Write the number of dots on each side of each domino. Do not draw dots.

Example

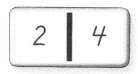

both even

both odd

one odd, one even

The two people who sorted dominoes with even and odd numbers of dots need their own Record Sheets. They should share the work.

3. Count the dominoes in each pile.

When you have finished this activity, give page 24 to your teacher.

Domino Sort **Record Sheet**

Circle the kind of domino you are sorting.

both even   **both odd**   **one odd, one even**

 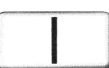 

  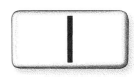

  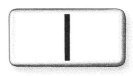

Copyright © SRA/McGraw-Hill

Use with Lesson 3.4.

Covering Shapes with Pattern Blocks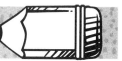

Cover each shape by using the pattern blocks in different ways. Then show what you did. Trace the blocks or use your Pattern-Block Template.

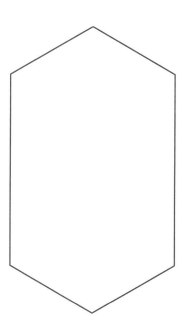 

Adapted from *Math Tools for Teachers*.
Use with Lesson 3.4.

25

Covering More Shapes

Cover each shape by using the pattern blocks in different ways. Then show what you did. Trace the blocks or use your Pattern-Block Template.

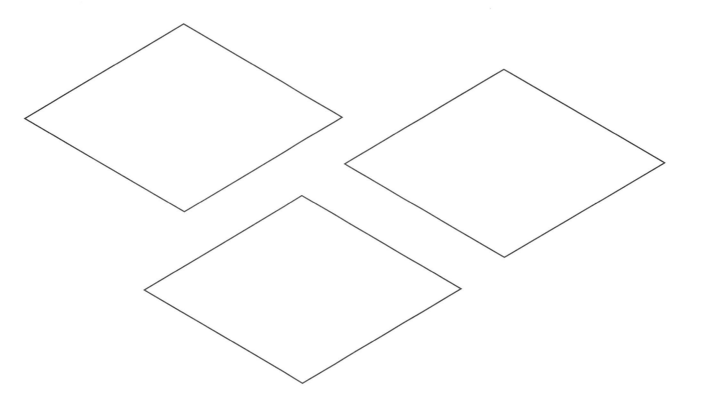

Use pattern blocks to make your own shape. Show what you did. Trace the blocks or use your Pattern-Block Template. Try to cover your shape in another way.

Adapted from *Math Tools for Teachers*.
Use with Lesson 3.4.

Name

Date

Number Line

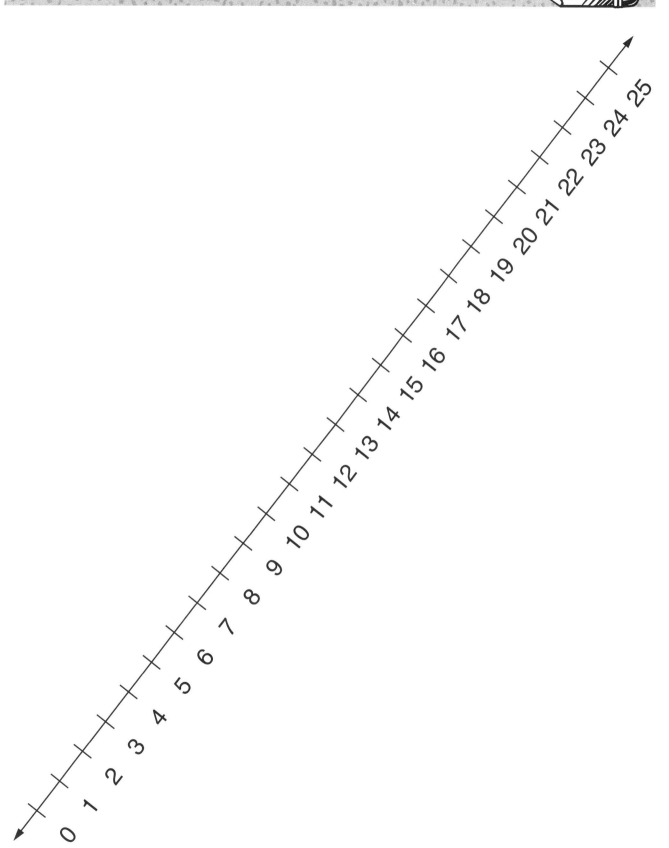

0 1 2 3 4 5 6 7 8 9 10 11 12 13 14 15 16 17 18 19 20 21 22 23 24 25

Use with Lesson 3.5.

Frames and Arrows

Complete the Frames-and-Arrows diagrams.

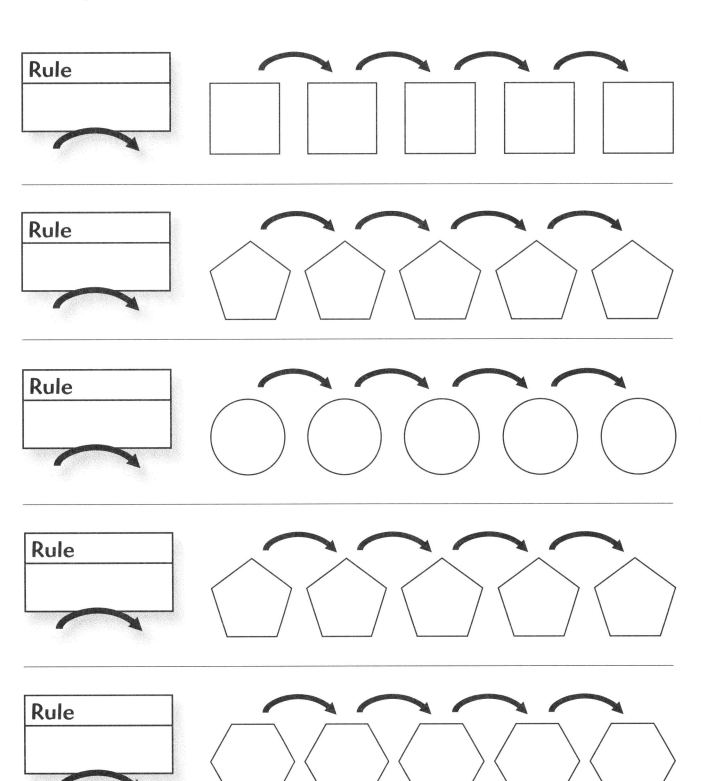

Use with Lesson 3.8.

Coin Exchanges Record

Grab a handful of pennies. Write the number of pennies you grabbed.

Trade as many of the pennies as you can for dimes. Trade as many of the leftover pennies as you can for nickels. Write the numbers of dimes, nickels, and pennies you have in the next 3 columns of the table.

Pennies Grabbed	Dimes	Nickels	Pennies

Dime-Nickel-Penny Grab

Play with 10 dimes, 8 nickels, and 20 pennies.

Mix the coins. One player grabs a handful. The other player takes what is left.

Round 1

I grabbed _____ Ⓓ, _____ Ⓝ, and _____ Ⓟ.

My partner grabbed _____ Ⓓ, _____ Ⓝ, and _____ Ⓟ.

I have _____ ¢. My partner has _____ ¢.

Who has more? _____

Round 2

I grabbed _____ Ⓓ, _____ Ⓝ, and _____ Ⓟ.

My partner grabbed _____ Ⓓ, _____ Ⓝ, and _____ Ⓟ.

I have _____ ¢. My partner has _____ ¢.

Who has more? _____

Round 3

I grabbed _____ Ⓓ, _____ Ⓝ, and _____ Ⓟ.

My partner grabbed _____ Ⓓ, _____ Ⓝ, and _____ Ⓟ.

I have _____ ¢. My partner has _____ ¢.

Who has more? _____

Use with Lesson 3.12.

Domino Cutouts

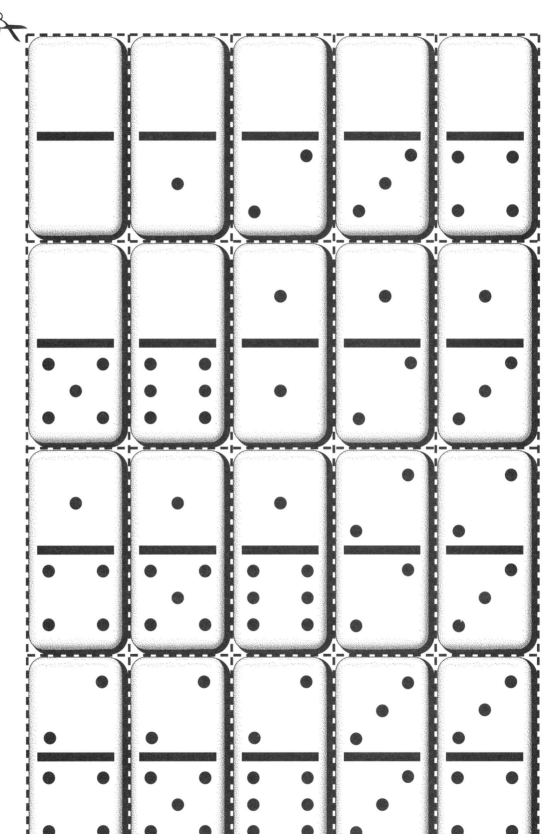

Use with Lesson 3.14.

31

Domino Cutouts (cont.)

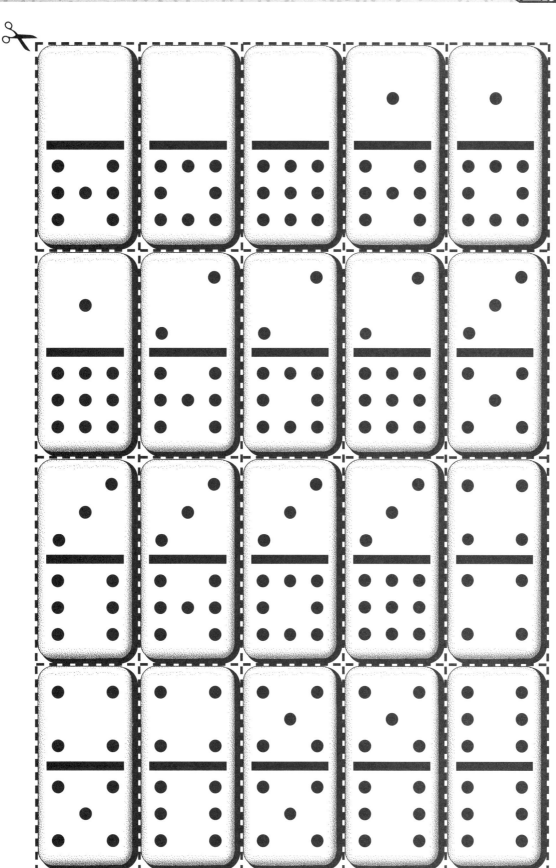

Use with Lesson 3.14.

Thermometer

°F

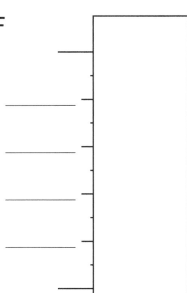

Write the temperature for each mercury strip.

A _____

B _____

C _____

D _____

E _____

F _____

G _____

H _____

Mercury Strips

Cut out the strips.

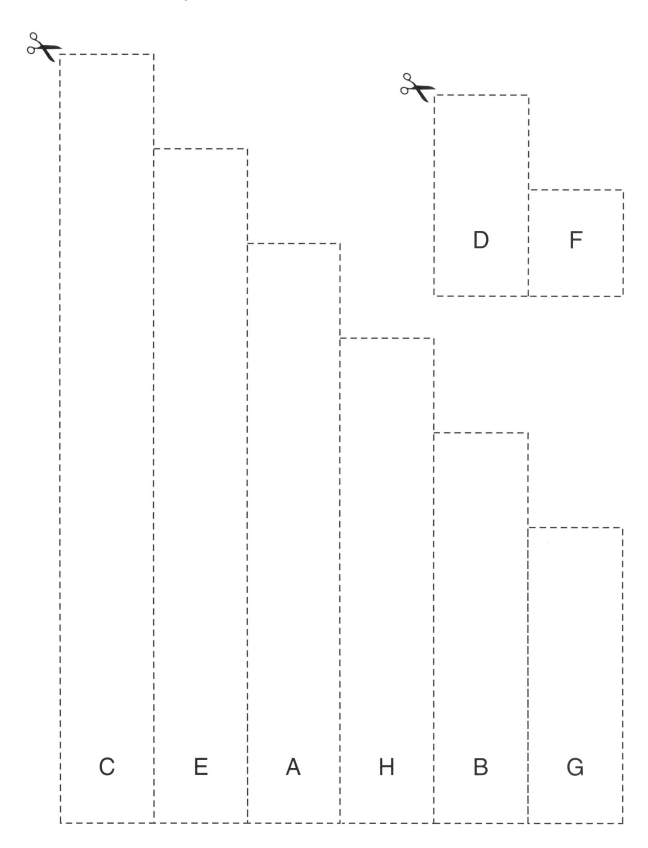

Use with Lesson 4.1.

Foot-Long Foot

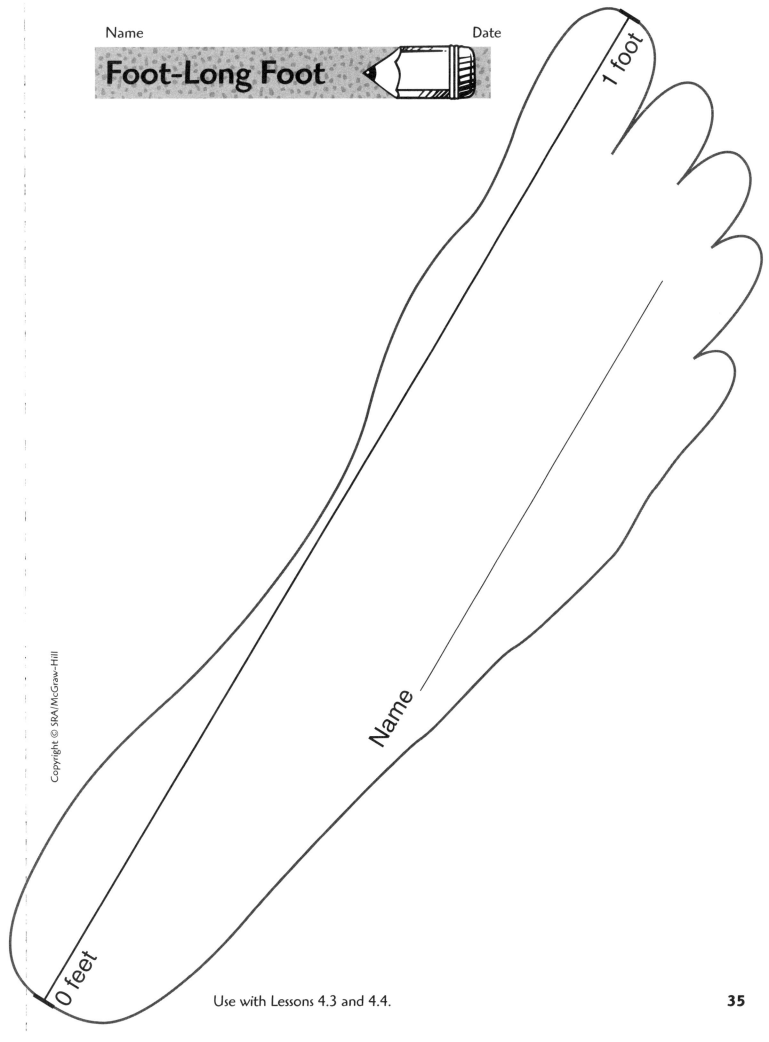

1 foot

Name

0 feet

Use with Lessons 4.3 and 4.4.

35

Name

Date

12-inch Ruler

0 INCHES 1 2 3 4 5 6 7 8 9 10 11 12

Use with Lesson 4.4.

Time Match Cards

Time Match Cards (cont.)

3 o'clock	6 o'clock	Half-past 11 o'clock
Half-past 4 o'clock	Half-past 2 o'clock	Half-past 10 o'clock
Half-past 12 o'clock	Quarter-past 5 o'clock	Quarter-before 7 o'clock
Half-past 6 o'clock	Half-past 8 o'clock	8 o'clock

Time Match Cards (cont.)

Quarter-past 9 o'clock	Quarter-before 3 o'clock	Quarter-to 11 o'clock
Quarter-to 9 o'clock	Quarter-after 4 o'clock	Quarter-after 1 o'clock

Use with Lesson 4.10.

6-Inch Rulers

Ruler 1: in. 0 1 2 3 4 5 6 / cm 0 1 2 3 4 5 6 7 8 9 10 11 12 13 14 15

Ruler 2: in. 0 1 2 3 4 5 6 / cm 0 1 2 3 4 5 6 7 8 9 10 11 12 13 14 15

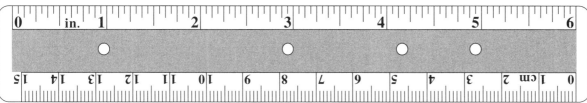

Ruler 3: in. 0 1 2 3 4 5 6 / cm 0 1 2 3 4 5 6 7 8 9 10 11 12 13 14 15

Use with Lesson 4.5.

Name   Date

Geoboard Dot Paper (5 × 5)

1.

2.

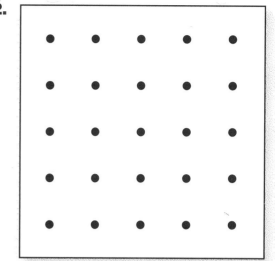

3.

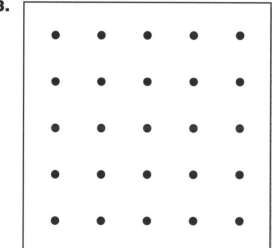

4.

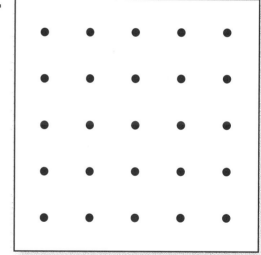

5.

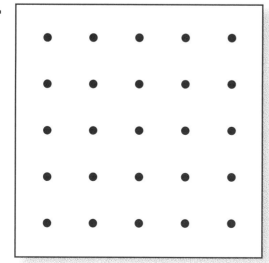

6.

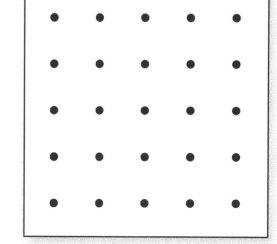

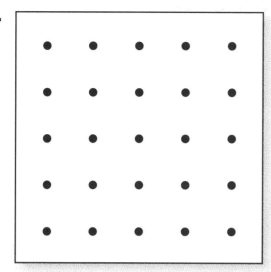

Use with Lesson 4.7.

Name   Date

1.

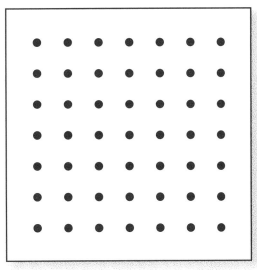

2.

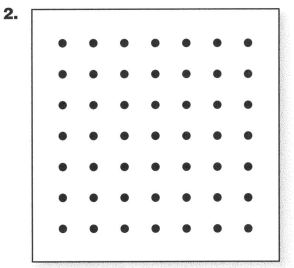

3.

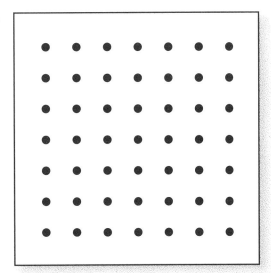

4.

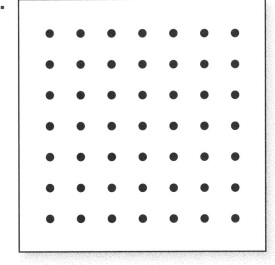

5.

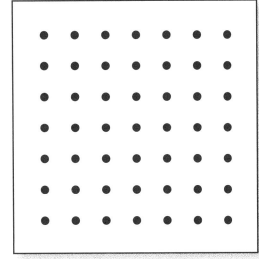

6.

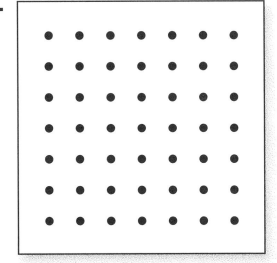

Use with Lesson 4.7.

Name   Date

Building with Base-10 Blocks

Flats	Longs	Cubes
2	8	4

✂ -

Name   Date

Building with Base-10 Blocks

Flats	Longs	Cubes
2	8	4

Copyright © SRA/McGraw–Hill

24-Hour Timeline

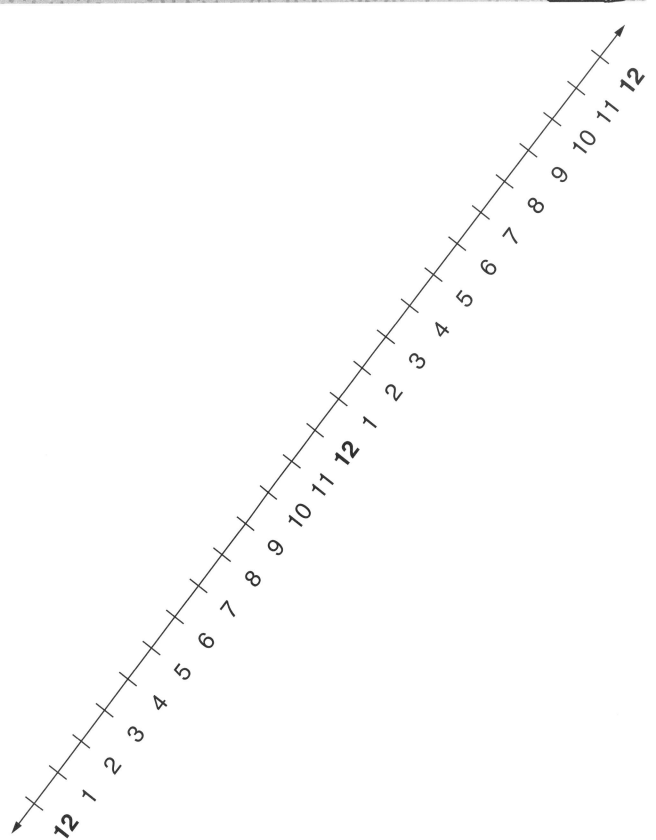

Use with Lesson 4.9.

Beginning Scroll Page

0											
−1											
−2											
−3											
−4											
−5											
−6											
−7											
−8											
−9											

Use with Lesson 4.10.

Continuing Scroll Page

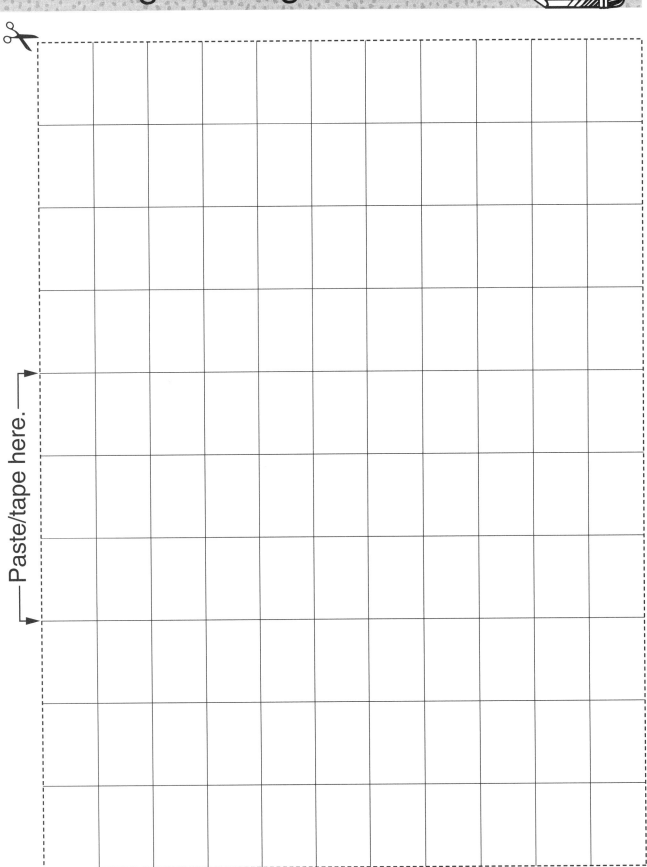

Paste/tape here.

Use with Lesson 4.10.

Negative-Number Scroll Page

										0
										-1
										-2
										-3
										-4
										-5
										-6
										-7
										-8
										-9

Base-10 Blocks

Base-10 Blocks

Cubes
1

Longs
10

Flats
100

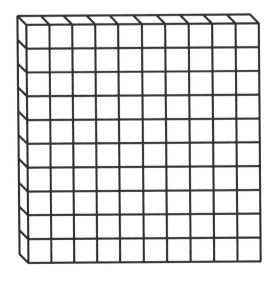

Use with Lesson 4.10.

Thermometer

✂   ✂

Color this red.
←

°F

120

110

100 — red

90 — orange

80

70 — yellow

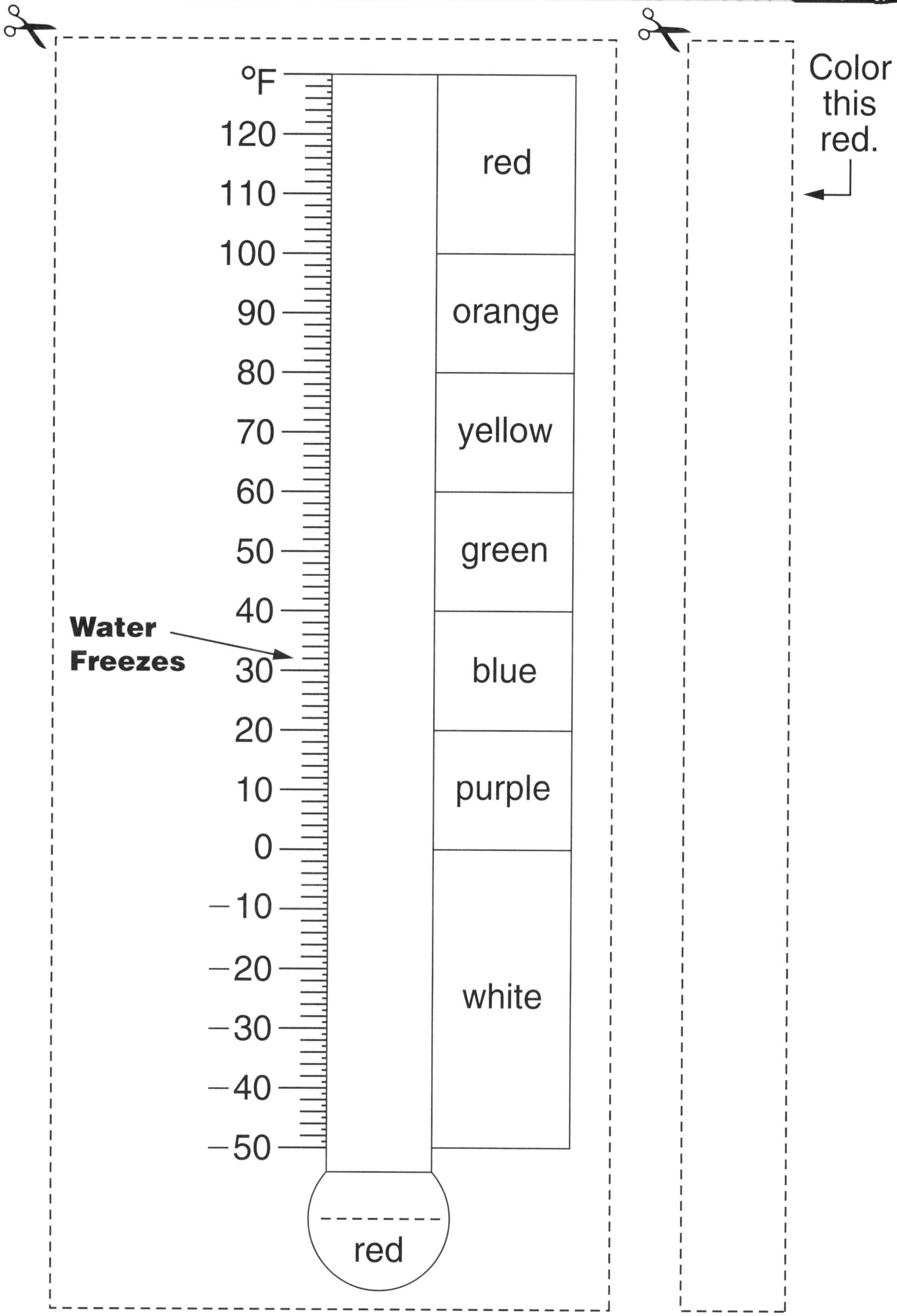

60

50 — green

40

Water Freezes → 30 — blue

20

10 — purple

0

−10

−20

−30 — white

−40

−50

red

Color by Number

Find the sums. If the sum is
- 7, color the space blue.
- 8, color the space red.
- 9, color the space green.
- 10, color the space black.

$$5 + 3 =$$

$$\begin{array}{r} 3 \\ + 4 \\ \hline \end{array}$$

$$2 + 5 = \underline{\quad}$$

$$7 + 0 = \underline{\quad}$$

$$4 + 3 = \underline{\quad}$$

$$\begin{array}{r} 6 \\ + 4 \\ \hline \end{array}$$

$$\begin{array}{r} 3 \\ + 7 \\ \hline \end{array}$$

$$5 + 4 = \underline{\quad}$$

$$\begin{array}{r} 5 \\ + 2 \\ \hline \end{array}$$

$$\begin{array}{r} 2 \\ + 8 \\ \hline \end{array}$$

$$\begin{array}{r} 5 \\ + 5 \\ \hline \end{array}$$

$$\begin{array}{r} 7 \\ + 2 \\ \hline \end{array}$$

$$\begin{array}{r} 4 \\ + 6 \\ \hline \end{array}$$

$$\begin{array}{r} 9 \\ + 1 \\ \hline \end{array}$$

$$\begin{array}{r} 8 \\ + 1 \\ \hline \end{array}$$

$$\begin{array}{r} 7 \\ + 3 \\ \hline \end{array}$$

$$\begin{array}{r} 0 \\ + 9 \\ \hline \end{array}$$

$$6 + 3 = \underline{\quad}$$

$$4 + 5 = \underline{\quad}$$

Use with Lesson 4.12.

Write Addition Facts

$$+ \,\square\!\square \over \square$$

$$+ \,\square\!\square \over \square$$

$$+ \,\square\!\square \over \square$$

$$+ \,\square\!\square \over \square$$

$$+ \,\square\!\square \over \square$$

$\square = \square + \square$ $\qquad$ $\square = \square + \square$ $\qquad$ $\square = \square + \square$

$\square + \square = \square$ $\qquad$ $\square + \square = \square$ $\qquad$ $\square + \square = \square$

$$+ \,\square\!\square \over \square$$

$$+ \,\square\!\square \over \square$$

$$+ \,\square\!\square \over \square$$

$$+ \,\square\!\square \over \square$$

$$+ \,\square\!\square \over \square$$

$\square = \square + \square$ $\qquad$ $\square = \square + \square$ $\qquad$ $\square = \square + \square$

$\square + \square = \square$ $\qquad$ $\square + \square = \square$ $\qquad$ $\square + \square = \square$

$$+ \,\square\!\square \over \square$$

$$+ \,\square\!\square \over \square$$

$$+ \,\square\!\square \over \square$$

$$+ \,\square\!\square \over \square$$

$$+ \,\square\!\square \over \square$$

Tens-and-Ones Mat

Tens 10s	Ones 1s

                    Use with Lesson 5.1.

Place-Value Mat

Hundreds	Tens	Ones

Relation Symbols

Use with Lesson 5.3.

Relation Symbols

<   means "is less than."

>   means "is more than."

=   means "is the same as."

=   means "is equal to."

Tabletop Area

Materials   ☐ "units" like same-size blocks, paper,
                   large floor tiles, or same-size books

                 ☐ a flat surface

                 ☐ slate

Work with the children in your group.

1. Choose a unit and a surface to cover.

Our unit: _____

Our surface: _____

2. Estimate how many units you need to cover the surface.

_____

3. Talk about your estimate with others in your group.

If you want to change your estimate, write it here.

_____

4. Cover the surface with units. Count the units.

Was your estimate close? _____

5. Cover the surface with a different unit.

Which of the two units is larger? _____

Did you need more of the larger
units or more of the smaller units? _____

Explore with the Pan Balance

Materials
- ☐ a pan balance
- ☐ sets of objects, such as pennies, base-10 blocks, pattern blocks, paper clips, unused pencils, new crayons

Place objects in the pans to make them balance.

1.

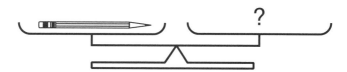

1 pencil _____ pennies

2.

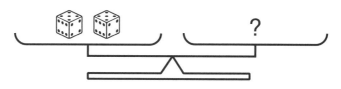

2 dice _____ cubes

Choose your own objects.

3.

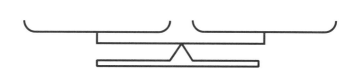

_____ _____

4.

_____ _____

Pile of Money

Materials   ❑ all your pennies and about
                      50 extra pennies

               ❑ slate

1. Count your pennies. Write the number on
   your slate.

2. Work with the children in your group. Put your
   pennies in a pile with everyone else's pennies.
   Add the extra pennies to the pile.

   Your job is to count the pennies in the pile.

   Before you start counting, make a plan.

   • How will you keep track of your pennies as
     you count?

   • Make sure everybody gets to count some
     pennies. How will you do that?

   • How will you check that your count is correct?

3. Record the final total on a quarter-sheet of paper.

4. Take back your pennies and put them in your
   tool kit.

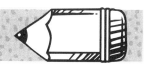

Area

Guess how many cubes are needed to cover each square.
Then cover each square with cubes to check your guess.

1. I think it will take

_____ cubes to
cover this square.

It took _____ cubes
to cover this square.

2. I think it will take

_____ cubes to
cover this square.

It took _____ cubes
to cover this square.

Use with Lesson 5.4.

Animal Posters

Cat
7 lb

Porpoise
98 lb

Use with Lesson 5.5.

Animal Posters

Cheetah
120 lb

Koala
19 lb

Animal Posters

Beaver
56 lb

Raccoon
23 lb

Animal Posters

Fox
14 lb

Rabbit
6 lb

Use with Lesson 5.5.

Animal Posters

First-Grade Girl

41 lb

8-year-old Boy

50 lb

Animal Posters

Eagle
15 lb

Penguin
75 lb

Comparing Animal Weights

Use your animal cards to complete the page.

Write **more** or **less** and < or >.

< is less than
> is more than

Example

Find the cat, the eagle, and the raccoon cards.

Unit
pounds

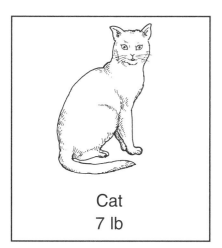

Cat
7 lb

Eagle
15 lb

Raccoon
23 lb

Together, the cat and the eagle weigh ___*less*___ than the raccoon.
        (**more** *or* **less**)

7 + 15 _____ 23
        (< *or* >)

1. Find the cat, the rabbit, and the eagle cards.

Together, the cat and the rabbit weigh _____ than the eagle.

7 + 6 _____ 15

Use with Lesson 5.6.

Comparing Animal Weights (cont.)

2. Find the rabbit, the fox, and the koala cards.

Together, the rabbit and the fox weigh _____ than the koala.

6 + 14 _____ 19

3. Find the boy, the beaver, and the cheetah cards.

Together, the boy and the beaver weigh _____ than the cheetah.

50 + 56 _____ 120

4. Find the raccoon, the fox, and the beaver cards.

Together, the raccoon and the fox weigh _____ than the beaver.

23 + 14 _____ 56

Challenge

5. Find the eagle, the fox, the girl, and the penguin cards.

Together, the eagle, the fox, and the girl weigh _____ than the penguin.

15 + 14 + 41 _____ 75

The *Difference Game*

Materials   ☐ number cards 1–10 (4 cards of each number)

☐ 40 pennies

Players   2

Directions

1. Mix the number cards. Put them facedown in a stack. Put 40 pennies in the bank.

2. To play a round, you and your partner:

• each take 1 card from the top of the deck

• each take the same number of pennies from the bank as you see on your card.

3. Find out how many more pennies one of you has than the other. Pair as many pennies as you can.

Here is an example.

Player A
Player B

4. The player with more pennies gets to keep the extra pennies.

The rest of the pennies go back in the bank.

5. The game is over when there are not enough pennies in the bank to play another round.

The player who took more pennies wins the game.

Comparing Coin Collections

1. Mike

Anna

Who has more money? _____ How much more? _____¢

---

2. Karen

Don

Who has more money?

How much more? _____¢

---

3. Ivan

Ⓟ Ⓟ Ⓓ Ⓟ Ⓓ Ⓟ Ⓓ Ⓓ

Jana

Ⓟ Ⓟ Ⓟ Ⓟ Ⓓ Ⓝ Ⓟ Ⓝ Ⓓ

Who has more money?

_____

How much more? _____¢

4. Lori

Ⓓ Ⓓ Ⓝ Ⓓ Ⓝ Ⓟ Ⓟ

Joe

Ⓝ Ⓝ Ⓓ Ⓓ Ⓟ Ⓟ Ⓟ Ⓓ Ⓟ

Who has more money?

_____

How much more? _____¢

Color by Number

5 + 6 = ____

3 + 5 = ____

____ = 8 + 3

4 + 6 = ____

7
+ 3
____

8 + 1 = ____

1
+ 8
____

0
+ 10
____

9
+ 2
____

8
+ 2
____

2
+ 7
____

____ = 2 + 6

6 + 3 = ____

6
+ 2
____

____ = 9 + 0

Use the color code to color the picture.

8 = yellow
9 = red
10 = green
11 = blue

Use with Lesson 5.9.

"What's My Rule?" 1

in   in   out

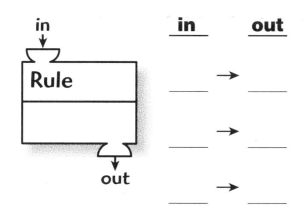

Rule

out

→
→
→
→
→
→

in   in   out

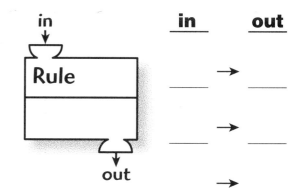

Rule

out

→
→
→
→
→
→

in   in   out

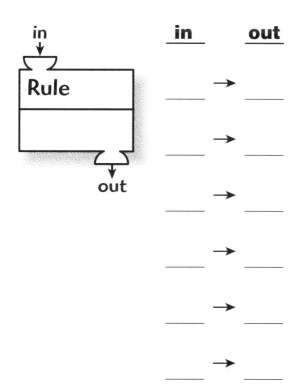

Rule

out

→
→
→
→
→
→

in   in   out

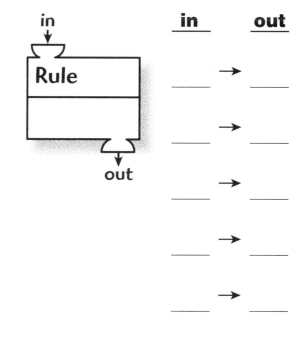

Rule

out

→
→
→
→
→
→

"What's My Rule?" 2

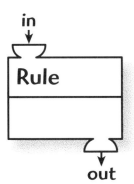

in	out

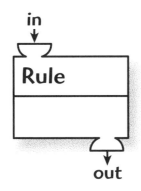

in	out

in
Rule
out

in	out

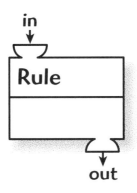

in	out

Use with Lesson 5.13.

Addition/Subtraction Facts Table

+, −	0	1	2	3	4	5	6	7	8	9
0	0	1	2	3	4	5	6	7	8	9
1	1	2	3	4	5	6	7	8	9	10
2	2	3	4	5	6	7	8	9	10	11
3	3	4	5	6	7	8	9	10	11	12
4	4	5	6	7	8	9	10	11	12	13
5	5	6	7	8	9	10	11	12	13	14
6	6	7	8	9	10	11	12	13	14	15
7	7	8	9	10	11	12	13	14	15	16
8	8	9	10	11	12	13	14	15	16	17
9	9	10	11	12	13	14	15	16	17	18

Using the Facts Table

+, −	0	1	2	3	4	5	6	7	8	9
0										
1										
2										
3										
4										
5										
6										
7										
8										
9										

         Use with Lesson 6.1.

Name-Collection Boxes

1.

2.

3.

4.

Use with Lesson 6.2.

Domino Totals

1. Find the total.

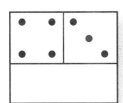

> **Unit**
> domino
> dots

Draw the missing dots.

2.
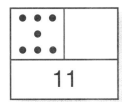
11

3.
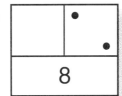
8

Use with Lesson 6.3.

✂ -

Domino Totals

1. Find the total.

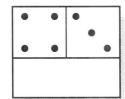

> **Unit**
> domino
> dots

Draw the missing dots.

2.
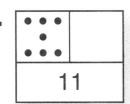
11

3.
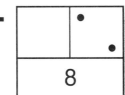
8

Use with Lesson 6.3.

Domino

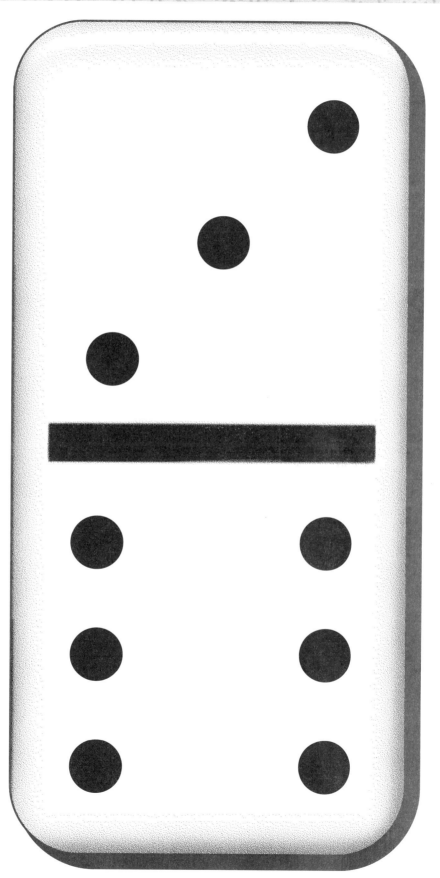

Use with Lesson 6.3.

Name

Date

Domino

Use with Lesson 6.3.

Fact Families

Write the 3 numbers for each domino.
Use the numbers to write the fact family.

1. Numbers: _____, _____, _____ [domino]

Fact family: ___ + ___ = ___   ___ − ___ = ___

___ + ___ = ___   ___ − ___ = ___

---

2. Numbers: _____, _____, _____ [domino]

Fact family: ___ + ___ = ___   ___ − ___ = ___

___ + ___ = ___   ___ − ___ = ___

---

3. Numbers: _____, _____, _____ [domino]

Fact family: ___ + ___ = ___   ___ − ___ = ___

___ + ___ = ___   ___ − ___ = ___

---

4. Make up your own domino. Draw the dots.

Numbers: _____, _____, _____

Fact family: ___ + ___ = ___   ___ − ___ = ___

___ + ___ = ___   ___ − ___ = ___

Fact Triangle

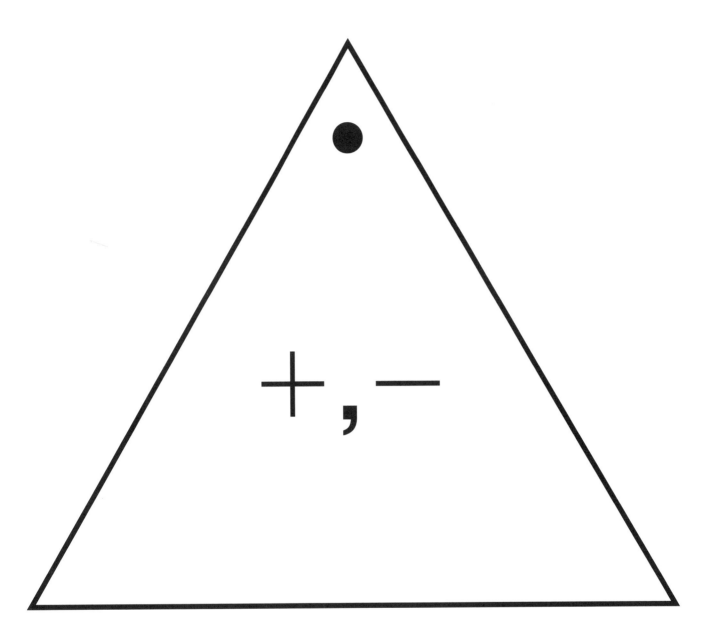

         Use with Lesson 6.4.

Fact Power Game Mat

START→	0 + 0	0 + 1	0 + 2	0 + 3	0 + 4	0 + 5	0 + 6	0 + 7	0 + 8	0 + 9
	1 + 0	1 + 1	1 + 2	1 + 3	1 + 4	1 + 5	1 + 6	1 + 7	1 + 8	1 + 9
	2 + 0	2 + 1	2 + 2	2 + 3	2 + 4	2 + 5	2 + 6	2 + 7	2 + 8	2 + 9
	3 + 0	3 + 1	3 + 2	3 + 3	3 + 4	3 + 5	3 + 6	3 + 7	3 + 8	3 + 9
	4 + 0	4 + 1	4 + 2	4 + 3	4 + 4	4 + 5	4 + 6	4 + 7	4 + 8	4 + 9
	5 + 0	5 + 1	5 + 2	5 + 3	5 + 4	5 + 5	5 + 6	5 + 7	5 + 8	5 + 9
	6 + 0	6 + 1	6 + 2	6 + 3	6 + 4	6 + 5	6 + 6	6 + 7	6 + 8	6 + 9
	7 + 0	7 + 1	7 + 2	7 + 3	7 + 4	7 + 5	7 + 6	7 + 7	7 + 8	7 + 9
	8 + 0	8 + 1	8 + 2	8 + 3	8 + 4	8 + 5	8 + 6	8 + 7	8 + 8	8 + 9
END→	9 + 0	9 + 1	9 + 2	9 + 3	9 + 4	9 + 5	9 + 6	9 + 7	9 + 8	9 + 9

Use with Lesson 6.4.

Fact Families and Fact Triangles

1.

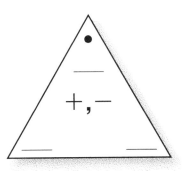

_____ + _____ = _____

_____ + _____ = _____

_____ − _____ = _____

_____ − _____ = _____

2.

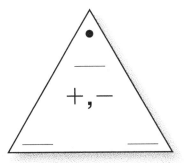

_____ + _____ = _____

_____ + _____ = _____

_____ − _____ = _____

_____ − _____ = _____

3.

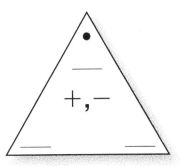

_____ + _____ = _____

_____ + _____ = _____

_____ − _____ = _____

_____ − _____ = _____

4.

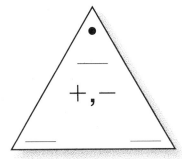

_____ + _____ = _____

_____ + _____ = _____

_____ − _____ = _____

_____ − _____ = _____

Use with Lesson 6.5.

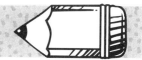

"What's My Rule?"

Use the Addition/Subtraction Facts Table to help you solve the following problems.

1.

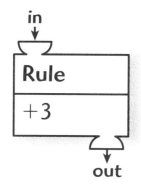

in	out
5	
7	
2	
9	
6	

2.

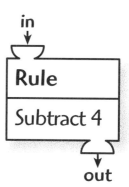

in	out
8	
10	
7	
4	
5	

3.

```
      in
       ↓
  ┌─────────────┐
  │ Rule        │
  ├─────────────┤
  │ Subtract 6  │
  └─────────────┘
       ↓
      out
```

in	out
14	
10	
12	
7	
15	

4.

```
      in
       ↓
  ┌─────────────┐
  │ Rule        │
  ├─────────────┤
  │ −5          │
  └─────────────┘
       ↓
      out
```

in	out
8	
12	
7	
5	
	9

Pattern-Block Play

Cover the larger block with smaller blocks. Use your template to show what you did.

1. 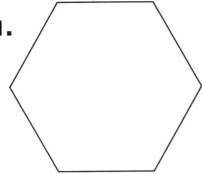 = _____

2. 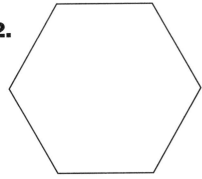 = _____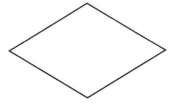

3. 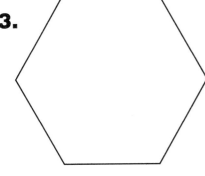 = _____

4. 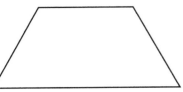 = _____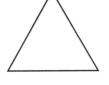

5. 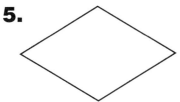 = _____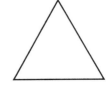

Use in Lesson 6.7.

Geoboard Triangles

1. Make a triangle that touches 4 pins. Copy your triangle below.

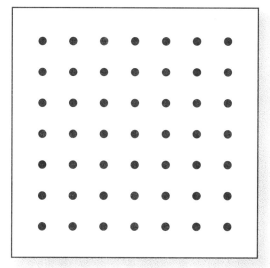

2. Make a different triangle that touches 4 pins. Copy it below.

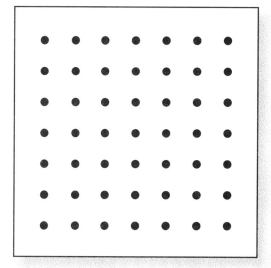

3. Make a triangle that touches 6 pins. Copy your triangle below.

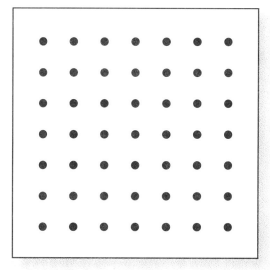

4. Make a different triangle that touches 6 pins. Copy it below.

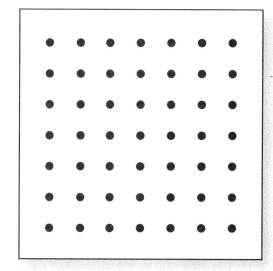

Analog and Digital Clocks

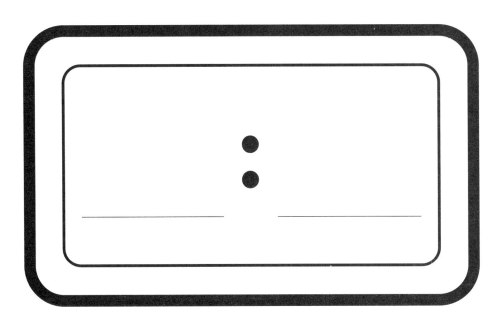

       Use with Lesson 6.10.

Time Match Cards

3:00	**6:00**	**11:30**
4:30	**2:30**	**10:30**
9:15	**5:15**	**6:45**
2:45	**8:30**	**8:00**

Use with Lesson 6.10.

Time Match Cards (cont.)

Use with Lesson 6.10.

Class Results of Calculator Counts

1. I counted to _____ in 15 seconds.

2. Class results:

Largest count	Smallest count	Middle number(s)	Range of class counts
_____	_____	_____	_____

3. Make a bar graph of the results.

Results of Calculator Counts

Number of Children

Counted to

Fact Triangles

Fact family:

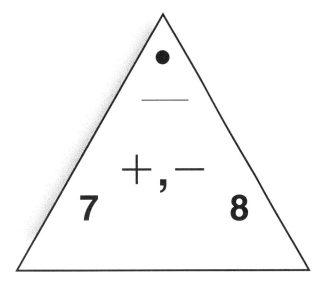

Use with Lesson 6.13.

✂ -

Name

Date

Fact Triangles

Fact family:

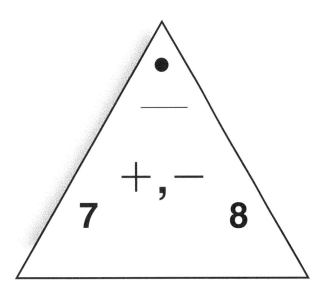

Use with Lesson 6.13.

Attribute Blocks: Size

Copy this design
using small blocks.
Trace your design.
Then color it to match
the blocks.

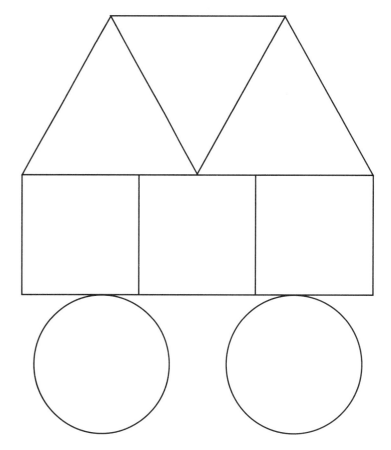

Make this design with large blocks on a desk or table.

Attribute Blocks: Color

Match blocks to this design. Use only one color.

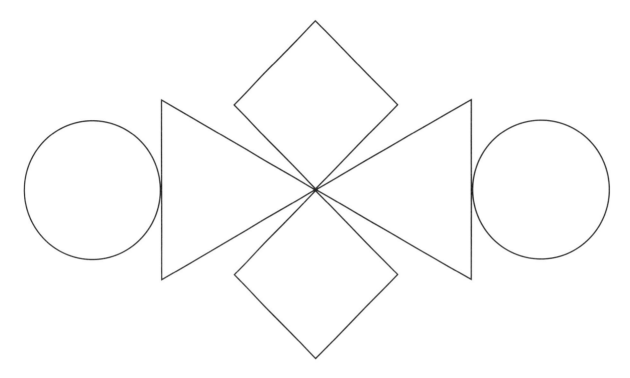

Make the above design with different-colored blocks.
Trace your design. Color it to match the blocks.

Fact Platter

Work with a partner.

Take turns.

One partner writes a "fact generator" inside the Fact Platter. For example: +5

The other partner writes the sums for that "fact generator" outside the Fact Platter.

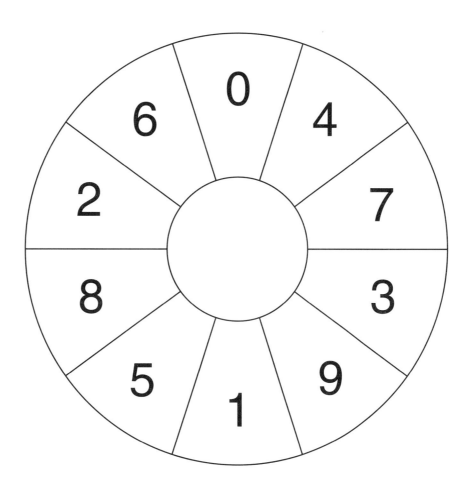

Polygons and Non-Polygons

These are polygons.

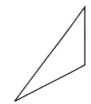 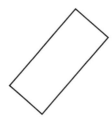 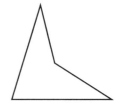

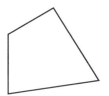   

  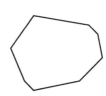

These are not polygons.

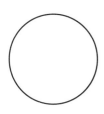 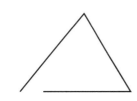 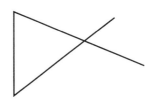

 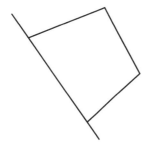 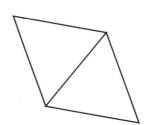 

Use with Lesson 7.4.

Bar Graph

3-Dimensional Shapes Poster

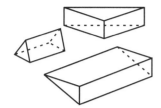
triangular prisms

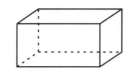
rectangular prisms

hexagonal prism

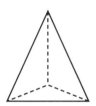
triangular pyramids

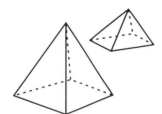
rectangular pyramids

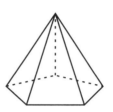
pentagonal pyramid

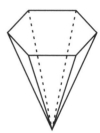
hexagonal pyramid

spheres

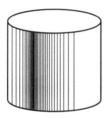
cylinders

cone

Five Regular Polyhedrons

The faces that make each shape are identical.

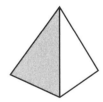
tetrahedron (pyramid) 4 faces

cube (prism) 6 faces

octahedron 8 faces

dodecahedron 12 faces

icosahedron 20 faces

Tens-and-Ones Trading Game

Materials
- ☐ a die
- ☐ base-10 blocks (longs and cubes)
- ☐ a Tens-and-Ones Mat (*Math Journal 1*, page 96) for each player

Players   2 or 3

Directions

Take turns rolling the die.

If you roll a 1, take 1 long.

If you roll a 2, take 2 longs.

If you roll a 3, take 3 cubes.

If you roll a 4, take 4 cubes.

If you roll a 5, take 5 cubes.

If you roll a 6, take 6 cubes.

Put your pieces on your Tens-and-Ones Mat. If you can, trade 10 cubes for 1 long. The first player to get 10 longs wins.

Another Way to Play

Place 10 longs on your Tens-and-Ones Mat. Take turns rolling the die and taking pieces off the mat. You must get the exact number to take the last pieces off. The winner is the first to take all the pieces off.

Heart Shape

Use with Lesson 7.7.

Coin Riddles

1. A candy bar costs 55¢. Use
exactly 3 coins to show
this amount.

2. Kelly spent $0.65 on a notebook.
Use exactly 5 coins to show
this amount.

Show the amount with fewer coins.

Challenge

3. Heather and Paul bought a kite
for 80¢. Heather paid $0.45. Paul
paid the rest. Use exactly 2 coins
to show the amount Paul paid.

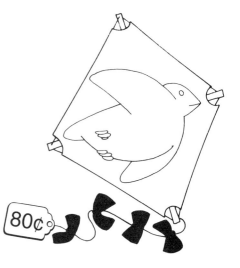

4. Make up a riddle of your own. On the back of this page,
draw a picture to show it.

$1 Bills

$1 Bills

Place-Value Mat

Dollars 100s Flats	Dimes 10s Longs	Pennies 1s Cubes
$1.00 100¢	$0.10 10¢	$0.01 1¢
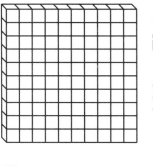		

Use with Lesson 8.3.

School Store Mini-Poster 2

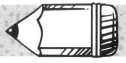

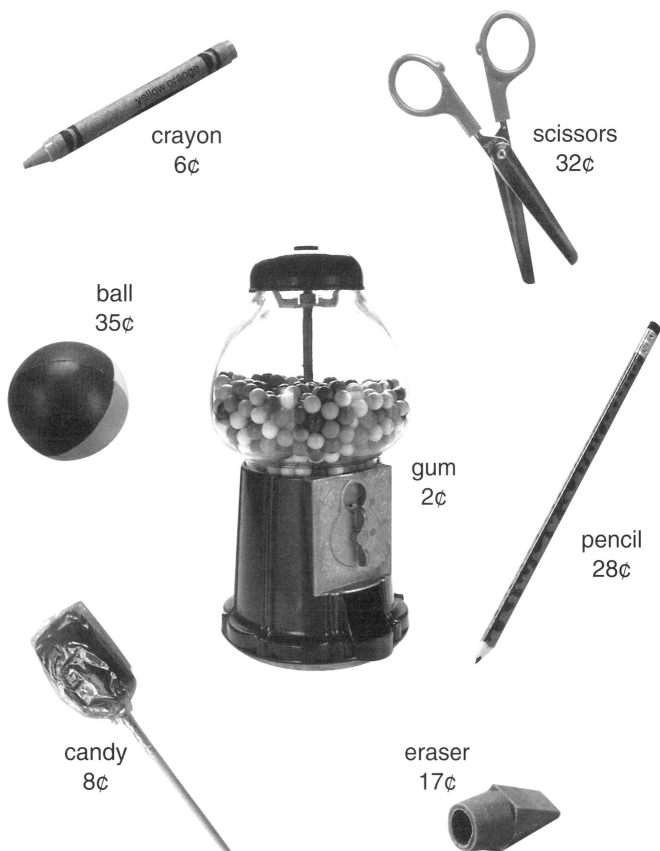

crayon
6¢

scissors
32¢

ball
35¢

gum
2¢

pencil
28¢

candy
8¢

eraser
17¢

School Store Mini-Poster 3

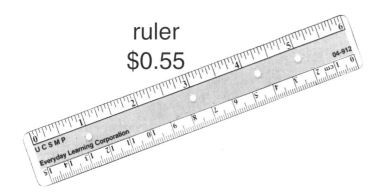

ruler
$0.55

glue
$0.84

stickers
23¢

LEARN
TO
READ

READ
TO
LEARN

pen
47¢

bookmark
12¢

crayons
$0.72

colored paper
$0.64 per pack

Museum Store Mini-Poster

seashell
48¢

kite
$1.86

elephant
72¢

rock
35¢

dinosaur
59¢

ring
18¢

magnet
$1.39

puzzle
85¢

plane
27¢

Buying Record

Name _____

I bought a _____.

It cost _____¢. I paid $1.

I received these coins in change. (Draw the coins.)

I received _____¢ in change.

Name _____

I bought a _____.

It cost _____¢. I paid $1.

I received these coins in change. (Draw the coins.)

I received _____¢ in change.

Name _____

I bought a _____.

It cost _____¢. I paid $1.

I received these coins in change. (Draw the coins.)

I received _____¢ in change.

Name _____

I bought a _____.

It cost _____¢. I paid $1.

I received these coins in change. (Draw the coins.)

I received _____¢ in change.

Use with Lesson 8.5.

Cracker Play

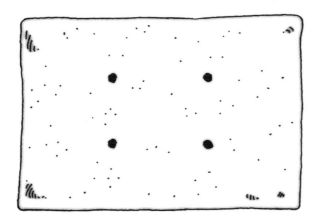

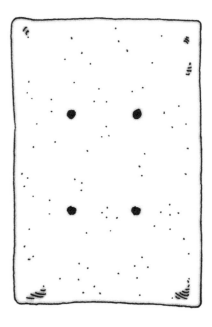

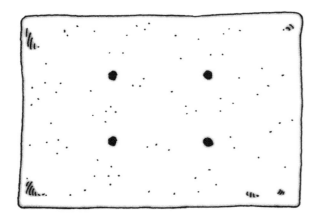

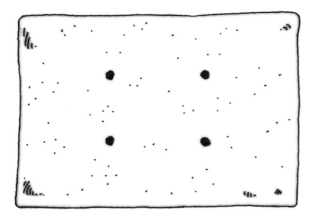

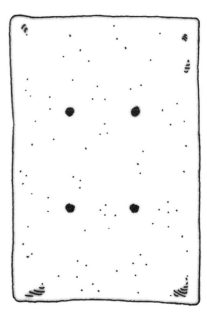

Name   Date

Fraction Book Pages

This object is divided into _____ equal parts.

I have shaded one of the equal parts.

I have shaded _____ of the object.

✂ --

Name   Date

Fraction Book Pages

This object is divided into _____ equal parts.

I have shaded one of the equal parts.

I have shaded _____ of the object.

Use with Lesson 8.7.

Pattern-Block Puzzles

Example

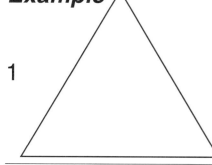 1 = __4__ 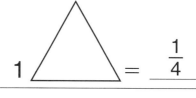 s

1 △ = __$\frac{1}{4}$__ of the large shape.

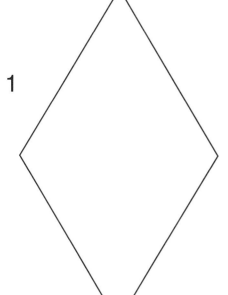 1 = _____ 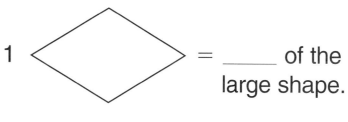 s

1 ⬦ = _____ of the large shape.

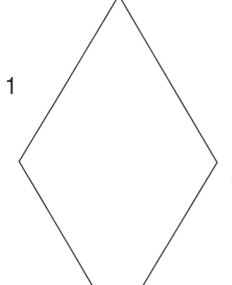 1 = _____ △ s

1 △ = _____ of the large shape.

Use with Lesson 8.9.   **109**

More Pattern-Block Puzzles

1 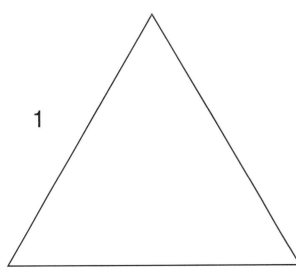 = _____ △ s

1 △ = _____ of the large shape.

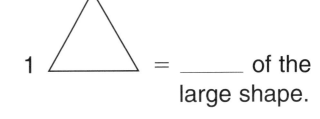

1 △ = _____ ⬭ s

1 ⬭ = _____ of the large shape.

You choose. Use one pattern block many times to make a large shape.

Each small shape is what fraction of the large shape? _____

Use with Lesson 8.9.

Fact-Triangle Sorting Record

Sort your Fact Triangles into doubles, near doubles, and 10 sums. Record each kind below. Then record the rest of your Fact Triangles.

Doubles

$2 + 2 = 4$

_____   _____   _____

_____   _____   _____

_____

Near Doubles

$2 + 3 = 5$

_____   _____   _____

_____   _____   _____

_____   _____   _____

_____   _____

10 Sums $2 + 8 = 10$

_____   _____   _____

Fact-Triangle Sorting Record (cont.)

Other Facts

2 + 4 = 6   _____   _____

_____   _____   _____

_____   _____   _____

_____   _____   _____

_____   _____   _____

_____   _____   _____

_____   _____   _____

_____   _____   _____

_____   _____

Which fact did you write more than once? _____

Use with Lesson 8.9.

Number Grid

									0
1	2	3	4	5	6	7	8	9	10
11	12	13	14	15	16	17	18	19	20
21	22	23	24	25	26	27	28	29	30
31	32	33	34	35	36	37	38	39	40
41	42	43	44	45	46	47	48	49	50
51	52	53	54	55	56	57	58	59	60
61	62	63	64	65	66	67	68	69	70
71	72	73	74	75	76	77	78	79	80
81	82	83	84	85	86	87	88	89	90
91	92	93	94	95	96	97	98	99	100
101	102	103	104	105	106	107	108	109	110

12-Cell Strip

glue   glue

Use with Lesson 9.1.

Framed Number Grid

									0
1	2	3	4	5	6	7	8	9	10
11									
21									
31									
41									
51									
61									
71									
81									
91									
101									

Blank Number Grid

Use with Lesson 9.1.

Number-Grid Pieces

Name _____

This is part of a number grid.
Fill in the missing numbers.

23

Name _____

This is part of a number grid.
Fill in the missing numbers.

23

Name _____

This is part of a number grid.
Fill in the missing numbers.

23

Name _____

This is part of a number grid.
Fill in the missing numbers.

23

Masks for Class Number Grid

Use with Lesson 9.3.

How Much a Container Holds

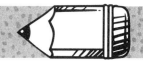

1. Fill the small cup to the top. Pour its contents into Container A. Repeat this until you have filled Container A to the top.

   Container A holds about _____ small cups.

2. Use the small cup to fill Container B and then Container C.

   Container B holds about _____ small cups.

   Container C holds about _____ small cups.

3. Draw the containers in order from smallest to largest. Use the back of this page.

4. Now use the large cup to fill each container.

   Container A holds about _____ large cups.

   Container B holds about _____ large cups.

   Container C holds about _____ large cups.

5. Do the containers hold more small cups or more large cups? _____

Pattern-Block Symmetry

Complete the design.
The two halves
should match.

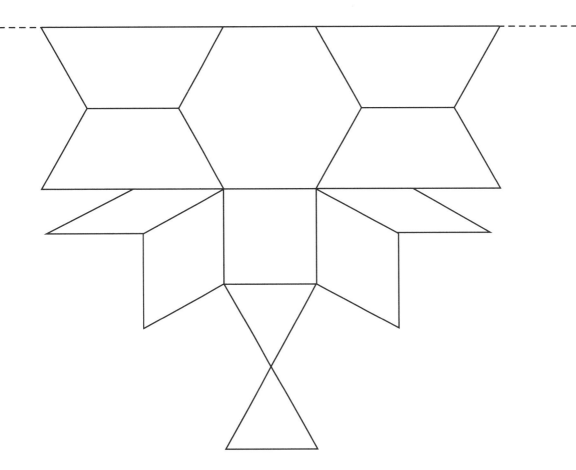

Use with Lesson 9.5.

Squares for Fractions

Fraction Strips

1-strip

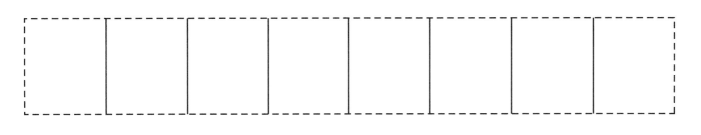

Use with Lesson 9.7.

Fractions and Pattern Blocks

Use your Pattern-Block Template to divide each of the hexagons into equal parts.

1. Show halves.   **2.** Show thirds.   **3.** Show sixths.

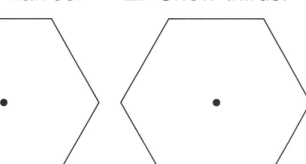

Use your template to draw each part.

4. Draw $\frac{1}{2}$ of a hexagon.

5. Draw $\frac{1}{3}$ of a hexagon.

6. Draw $\frac{1}{6}$ of a hexagon.

Use the hexagons in Problems 1–3 to help you solve the problems below. Write $<$, $>$, or $=$.

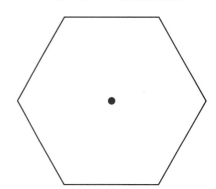

$<$ is less than

$>$ is greater than

$=$ is equal to

7. $\frac{1}{2}$ ——— $\frac{1}{3}$ **8.** $\frac{1}{6}$ ——— $\frac{1}{2}$ **9.** $\frac{1}{3}$ ——— $\frac{1}{6}$

10. $\frac{1}{2}$ ——— $\frac{2}{3}$ **11.** $\frac{1}{3}$ ——— $\frac{2}{6}$ **12.** $\frac{1}{2}$ ——— $\frac{3}{6}$

Deena's Mistake

Name _____

Deena filled in the number-grid puzzle. Finish the puzzle. Find her mistake. Cross out her mistake and write the correct number next to it.

	37
	47
	67
77	

Name _____

Deena filled in the number-grid puzzle. Finish the puzzle. Find her mistake. Cross out her mistake and write the correct number next to it.

	37
	47
	67
77	

Name _____

Deena filled in the number-grid puzzle. Finish the puzzle. Find her mistake. Cross out her mistake and write the correct number next to it.

	37
	47
	67
77	

Name _____

Deena filled in the number-grid puzzle. Finish the puzzle. Find her mistake. Cross out her mistake and write the correct number next to it.

	37
	47
	67
77	

Use with Lesson 9.9.

Time Match Cards

| 2:10 | 5:25 | 10:35 |

| 4:55 | 7:20 | 9:40 |

Vending Machine

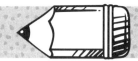

Use with Lesson 10.3.

Place-Value Mat for $1, $10, $100

One Dollar **$1** **100 pennies** **10 dimes**	
Ten Dollars **$10** **1,000 pennies** **100 dimes**	
One Hundred Dollars **$100** **10,000 pennies** **1,000 dimes**	

$10 and $100 Bills

Use with Lesson 10.3.

License-Plate Digits Report

Take out your number cards 0, 1, 2, 3, 4, and 5. Use the cards to help you write license-plate numbers that total 5. Work with children in your group.

For each license-plate number, use a card only one time. For example, 1, 1, 3, will not work because you can use the 1 card only once.

Examples

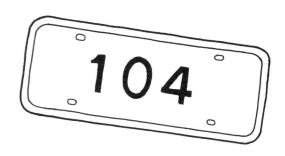

License-plate numbers:

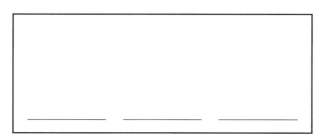

Home Link

Family Note

Family Letter

Fact Triangles 1

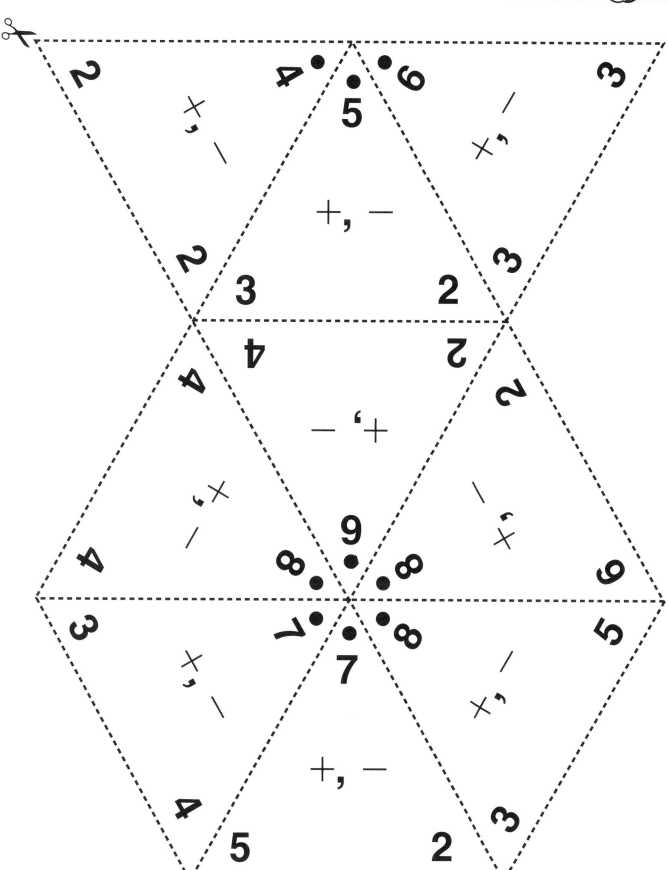

Fact Triangles 2

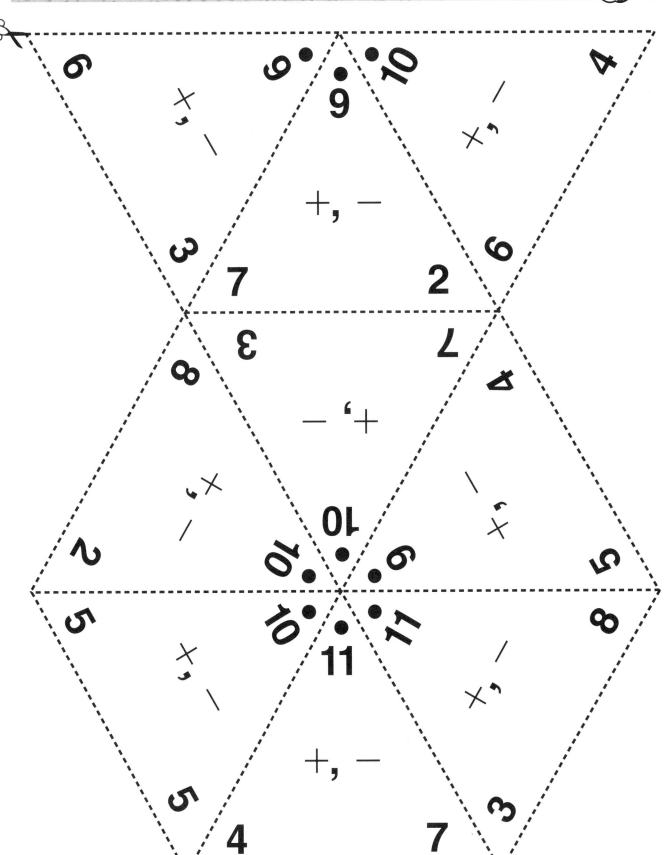

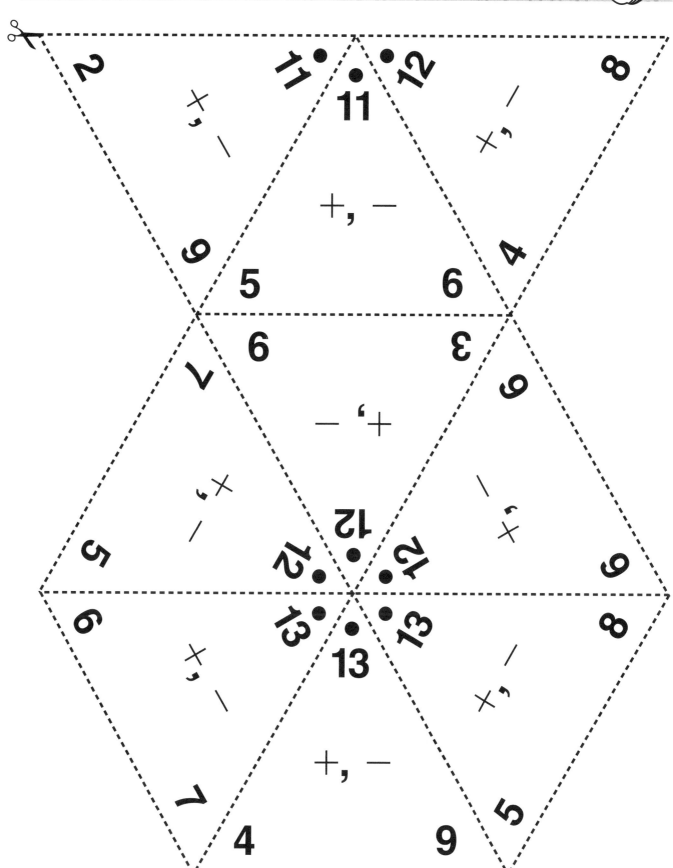

Fact Triangles 4

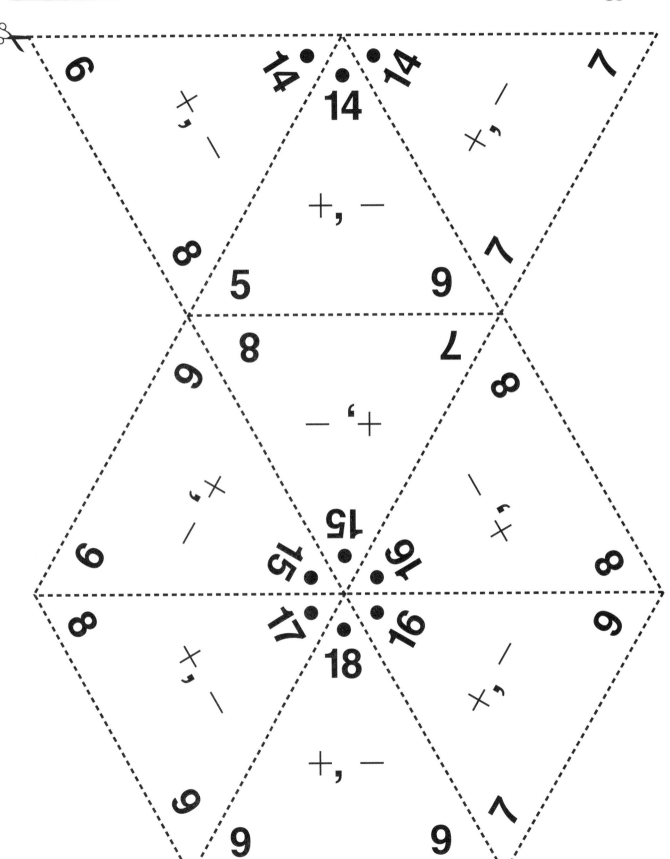

Family Letter

Introduction to First Grade Everyday Mathematics

Welcome to *First Grade Everyday Mathematics*. It is part of an elementary school mathematics curriculum developed by the University of Chicago School Mathematics Project (UCSMP). *Everyday Mathematics* offers children a broad background in mathematics.

Several features of the program are described below to help familiarize you with the structure and expectations of *Everyday Mathematics*.

A problem-solving approach based on everyday situations. By making connections between their own knowledge and their experiences in school and outside of school, children learn basic skills in meaningful contexts so that mathematics becomes "real."

Frequent practice of basic skills. Instead of practice presented in a single, tedious drill format, children practice basic skills in a variety of engaging ways. In addition to completing daily mixed review pages, patterning on the number grid, and working with addition and subtraction fact families in different formats, children will play games that are specifically designed to develop basic skills.

An instructional approach that revisits concepts regularly. To enhance the development of basic skills and concepts, children regularly revisit previously learned concepts and repeatedly practice skills encountered earlier. The lessons are designed to take advantage of previously learned concepts and skills and to build on them throughout the year instead of treating them as isolated bits of knowledge.

A curriculum that explores mathematical content beyond basic arithmetic. Mathematics standards in the United States, as well as around the world, indicate that basic arithmetic skills are only the beginning of the mathematical knowledge children will need as they develop critical thinking skills. In addition to basic arithmetic, *Everyday Mathematics* develops concepts and skills in the following topics—numeration; operations and computation; data and chance; geometry; measurement and reference frames; and patterns, functions, and algebra.

First Grade Everyday Mathematics emphasizes the following content:

- **Numeration** Counting; reading and writing numbers; investigating place value of whole numbers; exploring fractions and money.

- **Operations and Computation** Learning addition and subtraction facts, fact families, and extended facts; beginning informal work with properties of numbers and problem solving.

- **Data and Chance** Collecting, organizing, and displaying data using tables, charts, and graphs.

- **Geometry** Exploring 2- and 3-dimensional shapes.

- **Measurement and Reference Frames** Using tools to measure length, capacity (quarts, liters), and weight; using clocks, calendars, timelines, thermometers, and ordinal numbers.

- **Patterns, Functions, and Algebra** Exploring attributes, patterns, sequences, relations, and functions; finding missing numbers and rules in Frames-and-Arrows and "What's My Rule?" problems; studying properties of operations.

Everyday Mathematics will provide you with ample opportunities to monitor your child's progress and to participate in your child's mathematics experiences.

Throughout the year, you will receive Family Letters to keep you informed of the mathematical content your child will be studying in each unit. Each letter will include a vocabulary list, suggested *Do-Anytime Activities* for you and your child, and an answer guide to selected Home Link (homework) activities.

You will enjoy seeing your child's confidence and comprehension soar as he or she connects mathematics to everyday life.

We look forward to an exciting year!

Use with Lesson 1.1.

Unit 1: Establishing Routines

One purpose of this first unit is to help children become comfortable with a cooperative-learning environment while building mathematical concepts. Another purpose is to introduce and establish routines that will be used throughout this year and in the grades to come. This unit also reviews various mathematical concepts that were introduced in Kindergarten.

In Unit 1, children will review counting by 1s, 2s, 5s, and 10s. They will have opportunities to count and record numbers of various objects, such as hands, fingers, eyes, and ears. In addition, they will use pennies to count money, practice writing numbers, and begin to use a thermometer.

Vocabulary

Important terms in Unit 1:

Home Links Activities intended to promote follow-up and enrichment experiences at home. Each Home Link activity is identified by the following symbol:

tally count Marks used to keep track of an amount counted or other data collected over a period of time. Tallies serve as a model for children to represent numbers they can count and say but cannot yet write.

$\cancel{||||}\ |||$ is the tally count
for the number 8.

temperature scales Columns of numbers found on thermometers. Most thermometers have both a Fahrenheit scale and a Celsius scale.

tool kits Individual zippered bags or boxes used in the classroom. They contain a variety of items, such as rulers, pennies, and number cards, to help children understand mathematical ideas.

Telephone Numbers

Family Note

Work with your child on memorizing important telephone numbers, including any emergency daytime numbers other than your home number. Also, help your child find other examples of uses of numbers. These uses might include some or all of the following:

- Measurements of length, weight, volume, and so on
- Dates and times
- Tables
- Temperatures
- Counts
- Addresses and license plates
- Costs

Please return this Home Link to school tomorrow.

1. Write your area code and home telephone number.

(____ ____ ____) ____ ____ ____ – ____ ____ ____ ____

      (area code)   (telephone number)

2. Write an emergency number with the area code. This number could be for a relative or neighbor. It might be the number for the local police department.

(____ ____ ____) ____ ____ ____ – ____ ____ ____ ____

3. Write your first, second, and third names.

_____

4. Bring more examples of numbers to school.

Counting Up and Back

Family Note

To reinforce various types of counting, listen as your child counts by 1s and 10s. Children love to count for someone, and doing so provides wonderful practice in this essential first grade skill.

Please return this Home Link to school tomorrow.

1. Count for someone at home.
Count up by 1s, starting with 1. I counted to _____.

2. Count back by 1s. Start with 20 or
the highest number you can. I started with _____.

3. Count up by 10s. Start with 10. I counted to _____.

4. Count back by 10s. Start with 50 or
the highest number you can. I started with _____.

5. Explain to someone at home how to use the number grid
to help with counts.

									0
1	2	3	4	5	6	7	8	9	10
11	12	13	14	15	16	17	18	19	20
21	22	23	24	25	26	27	28	29	30
31	32	33	34	35	36	37	38	39	40
41	42	43	44	45	46	47	48	49	50
51	52	53	54	55	56	57	58	59	60
61	62	63	64	65	66	67	68	69	70
71	72	73	74	75	76	77	78	79	80
81	82	83	84	85	86	87	88	89	90
91	92	93	94	95	96	97	98	99	100
101	102	103	104	105	106	107	108	109	110

Two-Fisted Penny Addition

**Family
Note**

By playing *Two-Fisted Penny Addition,* you are helping your child build a foundation for learning the basic addition facts. Knowing the basic facts will be useful later on, when your child will be solving more difficult addition and subtraction problems mentally.

Please return this Home Link to school tomorrow.

Play *Two-Fisted Penny Addition* with someone at home:

• Put 10 pennies on the table.

• Grab some pennies with one hand.
  Pick up the rest with the other hand.

• On a piece of paper, draw 2 large circles to show hands.
  Place 1 pile of pennies in each circle.

• Count the pennies on each circle.

• Write how many pennies are on each circle.

• Take turns with your partner.

1. Start with 10 pennies.

Number of Pennies in One Hand	Number of Pennies in the Other Hand

2. Start with 15 pennies.

Number of Pennies in One Hand	Number of Pennies in the Other Hand

Numbers Before and After

Family Note

When working with "before" and "after" numbers in the table below, start with small numbers—up to 15. Then, if your child is doing well, increase the size of the numbers. Also, ask your child to suggest numbers to write in the middle column of the table.

Please return this Home Link to school tomorrow.

Ask someone to write a number in the middle column.

• Write the number that comes *after* that number.

• Write the number that comes *before* that number.

Try this with many different numbers.

Before	Number	After
Example 8	9	10

Use with Lesson 2.4.

Clocks and Watches

Family Note

Both analog clocks (clocks that have hour hands and minute hands) and digital clocks should be included in the tallies in the table below. In today's lesson, we observed what happens to the hour hand on an analog clock as the minute hand moves around the clock face. In the next lesson, we will practice telling the time when the minute hand is pointing to 12.

Please return this Home Link to school tomorrow.

Ask someone to help you find all of the clocks and watches in your home.

Record the numbers with tally marks.

	Tallies
Clocks	
Watches	

Total: _____

Draw a picture of the most interesting clock or watch you found. It might be interesting because of the way it looks or where it is located.

Telling Time to the Hour

**Family
Note**

We have just begun our work with telling time. Your child is working on telling time to the hour. Ask your child to show times on the hour on the paper clock, as in Part 1 below.

Please return this Home Link to school tomorrow, but keep your child's paper clock for future use.

1. Show your paper clock to someone at home.

- Show 3 o'clock.

- Show 11 o'clock.

- Ask someone to name an hour for you to show.

2. Record the time.

_____ o'clock

_____ o'clock

3. Draw the hour hand.

7 o'clock

1 o'clock

Use with Lesson 2.6.

Ordering Numbers

Family Note

Over the next few weeks, we will be "getting to know coins" in our class. In the next lesson, we will learn about pennies. Here is some background information: Abraham Lincoln appears on the HEADS side. The Lincoln Memorial is shown on the TAILS side.

   Your child is also learning how to order and compare numbers. Dominoes are a perfect tool for practicing this skill. If you have dominoes at home, you may want to play ordering games with your child. At first, use consecutive numbers like 1, 2, 3, and 4.

Please return this Home Link to school tomorrow.

1. Get a penny.

   • Who is on the HEADS side? _____

   • What is on the TAILS side? _____

2. Cut out the dominoes at the bottom of the page.

   • Count the total number of dots on each domino.

   • Put the dominoes in order from least to greatest number of dots.

   • Tape the dominoes in order on the back of this page.

   • Write the total number of dots under each domino.

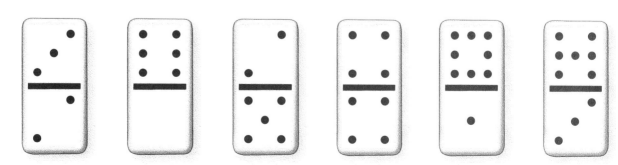

Name _____ Date _____

Nickels

Family Note

During the next few weeks, our class will learn about coins. For our next math lesson, your child will need 5 nickels. Please put these nickels in a sealed envelope with your child's name on it so that they will not get lost. (Your child will also need 10 dimes and 2 quarters in the coming days.)

Here is some background information about nickels: Thomas Jefferson appears on the HEADS side of the nickel. Monticello, Jefferson's home in Virginia, appears on the TAILS side.

Please return this Home Link to school tomorrow.

1. Ask someone at home for 5 nickels you can bring to school. Use one of them for this Home Link.

2. Look closely at a nickel. Ask someone to help you answer the following questions:

   • Who is on the HEADS side? _____

   • What is on the TAILS side? _____

3. Ask someone to trade you the correct number of pennies for your nickel.

   • How many pennies did the person give you?

     _____ pennies

   • How many pennies would you get for 2 nickels?

     _____ pennies

   • Explain to someone at home how you found your answer.

Use with Lesson 2.8.

Counting by 5s

Family Note

Counting by 5s is a useful skill for counting combinations of coins that include nickels. A good way to practice this skill is to count tally marks.

Please return this Home Link to school tomorrow.

1. Count by 5s for someone at home.

I counted up to _____.

2. Tell someone at home how many pennies you will get for 3 nickels.

3. Count the tally marks below.

~~HHT~~ ~~HHT~~ ~~HHT~~ ~~HHT~~ ~~HHT~~ ~~HHT~~ //

I counted _____ tally marks.

4. Draw some tally marks below.
Count them for someone at home.

I drew _____ tally marks.

Pennies and Nickels

Family Note

First graders do not always know how to represent an amount with the fewest number of coins. That's okay. At this stage, the important thing is that your child understands that 5 pennies can be exchanged for 1 nickel.

In a few days, we are going to set up a "store" in our classroom. Some children will take on the role of shopkeeper, others the role of shopper. Please send some old, inexpensive items (such as rulers, toy cars, stickers, or a ball and jacks) to school for us to use in our store. Thank you!

Please return this Home Link to school tomorrow.

1. Tell or show someone at home how many nickels you get for 10 pennies.

2. For each problem, write how much the coins are worth. Use Ⓟ and Ⓝ to show the amount with fewer coins.

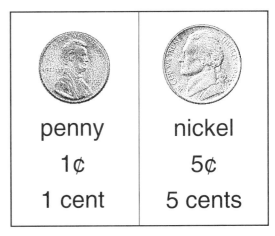

penny	nickel
1¢	5¢
1 cent	5 cents

Example Ⓟ Ⓟ Ⓟ Ⓟ Ⓟ Ⓟ Ⓟ is the same as
Ⓝ Ⓟ Ⓟ.

This is 7 cents.

a. Ⓟ Ⓟ Ⓟ Ⓟ Ⓟ Ⓟ Ⓟ Ⓟ Ⓟ Ⓟ Ⓟ is the same as

This is ____ cents.

b. Ⓝ Ⓟ Ⓟ Ⓟ Ⓟ Ⓟ Ⓟ is the same as

This is ____ cents.

Nickel/Penny Grab

Family Note

In class, we have been playing *Nickel/Penny Grab.* Ask your child to tell you how to play. The game provides practice in counting combinations of pennies and nickels and then comparing amounts of money. If your child is having trouble doing this, use real coins to model the problems. Another way to help your child is to trade nickels for pennies and then count the pennies.

We will be doing a lot of work with money exchanges and with counting money. But do not expect your child to master these skills at this time.

Please return this Home Link to school tomorrow.

Sabine and Tony played *Nickel/Penny Grab.*
They played 3 games. Here is what happened:

Game 1: Sabine grabbed 2 nickels and 7 pennies.

She had _____ ¢.

Tony grabbed 3 nickels and 1 penny. He had _____ ¢.

Circle who grabbed more: **Sabine** *or* **Tony**

Game 2: Sabine grabbed 2 nickels and 6 pennies.

She had _____ ¢.

Tony grabbed 3 nickels and 5 pennies. He had _____ ¢.

Circle who grabbed more: **Sabine** *or* **Tony**

Game 3: Sabine grabbed 4 nickels and 8 pennies.

She had _____ ¢.

Tony grabbed 3 nickels and 10 pennies. He had _____ ¢.

Circle who grabbed more: **Sabine** *or* **Tony**

Telling Time

Family Note

We have not practiced telling time in class for several days, so your child may need some review. Use the paper clock that your child brought home several days ago to practice telling time. If you no longer have the paper clock, you might use a small real clock instead.

Please return this Home Link to school tomorrow.

1. Record the time.

_____ o'clock

_____ o'clock

2. Draw the hour hand.

3:00

6:00

3. On the back of this page, draw a picture of something you will do at home tonight. Have someone help you figure out about what time (to the nearest hour) you will do the activity. Show the time on your paper clock.

Counting Money

Family Note

This Home Link may be challenging for your child. It not only reviews some of the concepts we have covered in this unit, but it also requires your child to apply these concepts to new situations. Do not worry if this page is challenging—we will be working on counting money throughout the year. Encourage your child to use real coins to model the problems.

Please return this Home Link to school tomorrow.

1. Have someone at home help you collect a small container of pennies and nickels. Take a handful of the coins.

2. How many coins are in one handful? How much are they worth?

   _____ pennies = _____¢   _____ nickels = _____¢

3. How much are the pennies and nickels worth together?

   I counted _____¢ in one handful.

4. Circle two items that you would like to buy.

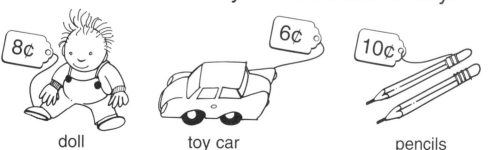

8¢   doll   6¢   toy car   10¢   pencils   3¢   sticker

   a. Which item costs more? _____

   b. How much more does it cost? _____¢ more

Challenge

5. How much do the two items cost together? _____¢

Family Letter

Unit 3: Visual Patterns, Number Patterns, and Counting

Children will have several experiences with patterns that use objects, colors, and numbers.

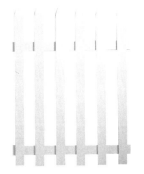

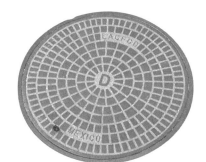

Count by 10s.	0, 10, 20
Count by 5s.	0, 5, 10, 15, 20
Count by 2s.	0, 2, 4, 6, 8, 10
Count by 3s.	0, 3, 6, 9, 12

*2, 4, 6, 8, 10, 12.
12 is an even number.*

As patterns with numbers are investigated, children will take a closer look at the common patterns found in odd and even numbers. They will observe the patterns in the ending digits of counts by 2s, 3s, 5s, and 10s. Frames-and-Arrows diagrams will be introduced to help children in their investigation of number sequences. (See explanation on next page.)

Children will also continue to develop their time-telling and money-counting skills. They will practice telling time on the hour and the half-hour. And they will continue to work with real coins, so we would like you to send 10 dimes to school to add to your child's tool-kit coin collection. (As before, please be sure to send these coins in a sealed envelope with your child's name on it.)

Finally, we will begin work on addition and subtraction. This is an important topic—it will be developed throughout the year. It is not too early for children to begin solving some very simple problems.

Use with Lesson 2.14.

Vocabulary

Important terms in Unit 3:

number grid A table in which consecutive numbers are usually arranged in rows of ten.

									0
1	2	3	4	5	6	7	8	9	10
11	12	13	14	15	16	17	18	19	20
21	22	23	24	25	26	27	28	29	30
31	32	33	34	35	36	37	38	39	40
41	42	43	44	45	46	47	48	49	50

Number grids are used to develop place-value concepts and addition and subtraction problem-solving strategies.

pattern A predictable arrangement of items.

even number Any whole number that ends in 0, 2, 4, 6, or 8. An even number of objects can always be broken into pairs.

odd number Any whole number that ends in 1, 3, 5, 7, or 9. When an odd number of objects is broken into pairs, there will always be one object that cannot be paired.

Frames and Arrows Diagrams that are used to represent number sequences or sets of numbers that are ordered according to a rule. Each frame contains one of the numbers in the sequence. Each arrow stands for the rule that tells which number goes in the next frame.

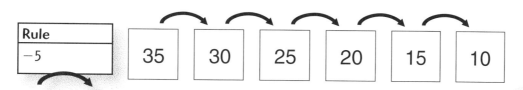

The Family Note on Home Link 3.8, which you will receive later, provides a more detailed description of Frames and Arrows.

Use with Lesson 2.14.

Do-Anytime Activities

To work with your child on concepts taught in this unit and in previous units, try these interesting and rewarding activities:

1 Count and pair objects found around the house and determine whether there's an odd or even number of items.

2 Using the same collection of objects, arrange them to make an ongoing pattern. Then have your child make and describe his or her own pattern.

3 Using the number grid, select a number and have your child point to the number that is 1 more or 1 less than the selected number. Do problems like this: "Start at 28. Count back (or up) 5 spaces. On which number do you land?"

Counting back from 28

									0
1	2	3	4	5	6	7	8	9	10
11	12	13	14	15	16	17	18	19	20
21	22	23	24	25	26	27	28	29	30
31	32	33	34	35	36	37	38	39	40
41	42	43	44	45	46	47	48	49	50

Use with Lesson 2.14.

As You Help Your Child with Homework

As your child brings home assignments, you may want to go over the instructions together, clarifying them as necessary. The answers listed below will guide you through this unit's Home Links.

Home Link 3.3

1. 6   **2.** 7   **3.** 10   **4.** 15   **5.** 14

Home Link 3.6

1. 7   **2.** 7   **3.** 5   **4.** 16

5. 10   **6.** 1   **7.** 12   **8.** 2

Home Link 3.7

1. 5 o'clock, 7 o'clock

2. half-past 2 o'clock, half-past 9 o'clock

Home Link 3.8

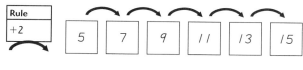

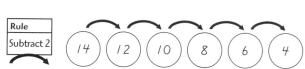

Home Link 3.9

Home Link 3.10

1. Franklin Roosevelt

2. A torch, a laurel, and an oak

3. 5 Ⓟ = 1 Ⓝ; 2 Ⓝ = 1 Ⓓ; 10 Ⓟ = 1 Ⓓ

4. 13¢; 19¢; 30¢

Home Link 3.11

3. Ⓓ; This is 10 cents.

4. Ⓓ Ⓟ Ⓟ; This is 12 cents.

5. Ⓓ Ⓟ Ⓟ Ⓟ Ⓟ; This is 14 cents.

6. Ⓓ Ⓓ Ⓝ; This is 25 cents.

7. Ⓓ Ⓓ; This is 20 cents.

Home Link 3.12

1. 25¢, or $0.25   **2.** 45¢, or $0.45   **3.** 23¢, or $0.23

4. 37¢, or $0.37   **5.** 43¢, or $0.43

Home Link 3.13

2a. blue   **2b.** yellow

Use with Lesson 2.14.

Patterns

Family Note

Patterns are so important in mathematics that mathematics is sometimes called the "Science of Patterns." Help your child identify patterns in and around your home and in the outside world.

Some suggestions for places to look for patterns:

· floor tiles   · carpeting   · window panes

· curtains   · wallpaper   · fences

Please return this Home Link to school tomorrow.

1. Find at least two patterns in your home. Draw the patterns you find.

2. If you have articles of clothing (such as a shirt or a pair of socks) that have patterns on them, please wear those clothes to school tomorrow!

                                                  Use with Lesson 3.1.

Name _____   Date _____

Odd and Even Numbers

Family Note

As children learn about the concept of odd and even numbers, extend this activity to include the number of people at home or the numbers of various objects, such as chairs, windows, videos, and books on a shelf.

Please return this Home Link to school tomorrow.

1. Count the number of people in your home.

There are _____ people in my home.

Is this number **even** or **odd**? _____

2. Tell someone at home about odd and even numbers.

Write some **odd** numbers here: _____, _____, _____, _____

Write some **even** numbers here: _____, _____, _____, _____

3. Count the number of a type of object in your home.
Write the number and the type of object.

There are _____ _____ in my home.

Is this number **even** or **odd**? _____

Copyright © SRA/McGraw-Hill

Number-Line Hops

Family Note

We are beginning to use the number line as a tool for solving addition and subtraction problems. Help your child answer the questions below by moving a finger from number to number on the number line. Make sure that your child is counting the number of hops and not the numbers themselves.

Please return this Home Link to school tomorrow.

Use the number line on the side of this page to help you answer the questions.

Example

Start at 5. Count the hops to 11. How many hops? __6__

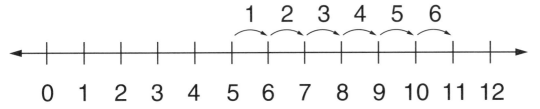

1. How many hops from 4 to 10? _____

2. How many hops from 8 to 15? _____

3. How many hops from 9 to 19? _____

4. How many hops from 1 to 16? _____

Challenge

5. Start at 3. Go 11 hops. Where do you end up? _____

6. If you go 7 hops and land on 14, where did you start? _____

0
1
2
3
4
5
6
7
8
9
10
11
12
13
14
15
16
17
18
19
20
21
22
23
24
25

More Odd and Even Numbers

Family Note

In class we are learning to identify even and odd numbers by looking at the last digit in a number. All even numbers end in 0, 2, 4, 6, or 8. All odd numbers end in 1, 3, 5, 7, or 9. Ask your child to explain how to tell whether a number is even or odd. Give examples of odd and even numbers for your child to identify.

Please return this Home Link to school tomorrow.

1. Write the number part of your address below.

_____

Is this number **odd** or **even**? _____

Tell someone you know.

2. Are the addresses across the street odd or even?

_____

3. Write an even number less than 50. Show it with tally marks.

_____

4. Write an odd number less than 50. Show it with tally marks

_____

Challenge

5. Write the biggest even number you know. _____

Ask or tell someone how to read this number.

Number Lines and Counting

Family Note

Listen as your child tells you about number lines and counts. Be sure he or she records the numbers counted. Provide several objects, such as pennies or dried beans, for your child to use to count by 10s, 5s, 2s, and 3s.

Please return this Home Link to school tomorrow.

Tell someone at home what you know about number lines and counting patterns.

Count by 10s, 5s, 2s, and 3s. Begin at 0 each time.

Then go back and circle all the odd numbers on the number line.

Count by 10s. 0, _____, _____

Count by 5s. 0, _____, _____, _____, _____

Count by 2s. 0, _____, _____, _____, _____

Count by 3s. 0, _____, _____, _____, _____

Use with Lesson 3.5.

More Number-Line Hops

Family Note

We are beginning to work with number models like 3 + 2 = 5 and 8 − 5 = 3. We are solving them by counting up and back on the number line. Ask your child to show you how to do this. If your child has trouble with the Challenge problems, make up number stories that use these numbers. For example, for 7 + 3 = ____, you might make up the following story: "You have 7 pennies. I give you 3 more. How many pennies do you have now?" Your child can use real pennies to find the answer.

Please return this Home Link to school tomorrow.

Use the number line to help you solve these problems.

1. Start at 4. Count up 3 hops. Where do you

end up? _____   4 + 3 = _____

2. Start at 12. Count back 5 hops. Where do you

end up? _____   12 − 5 = _____

3. Start at 11. Count back 6 hops. Where do you

end up? _____   11 − 6 = _____

4. Start at 14. Count up 2 hops. Where do you

end up? _____   14 + 2 = _____

Challenge

5. 7 + 3 = _____   **6.** 6 − 5 = _____

7. 2 + 10 = _____   **8.** 9 − 7 = _____

0
1
2
3
4
5
6
7
8
9
10
11
12
13
14
15
16
17
18
19
20
21
22
23
24
25

Telling Time to the Half-Hour

Family Note

We have just begun working on telling time to the nearest half-hour. Help your child complete these pages. Tell your child at which times, on the hour or half-hour, he or she wakes up and goes to bed on school days. We will continue to practice telling time at school. Have your child tell the time at home when it is close to the hour or half-hour.

Please return these Home Link pages to school tomorrow.

1. Record the time.

_____ o'clock

half-past _____ o'clock

half-past _____ o'clock

half-past _____ o'clock

Use with Lesson 3.7.

Telling Time (cont.)

Challenge

2. Draw the hour hand and the minute hand to show the time.

This is the time I wake up in the morning on a school day.

This is the time I go to bed at night before a school day.

Use with Lesson 3.7.

Frames-and-Arrows Diagrams

Family Note

Your child is bringing home an activity you may not be familiar with. It is called "Frames and Arrows."

    Frames-and-Arrows diagrams are used with sequences of numbers that follow one after the other according to a special rule. Frames-and-Arrows diagrams are made up of shapes, called **frames,** that are connected by **arrows.** Each frame contains one of the numbers in the sequence. Each arrow stands for the rule that tells how to find which number goes in the next frame. Here is an example of a Frames-and-Arrows diagram:

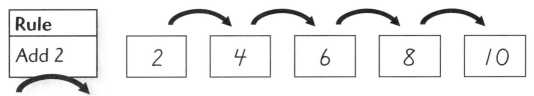

- The arrow rule is "Add 2" or "Count by 2s."

- In a Frames-and-Arrows problem, some of the information is left out. To solve the problem, you have to find the missing information.

Following are two examples of Frames-and-Arrows problems.

Example 1: Fill in the empty frames according to the arrow rule.

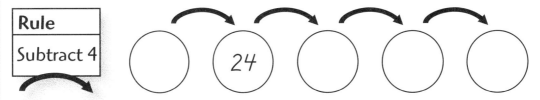

- **Solution:** Write 28 in the first empty frame and 20, 16, and 12 in the frames that follow.

Example 2: Write the arrow rule in the empty box.

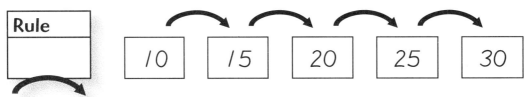

- **Solution:** The arrow rule is "Add 5" or "Count by 5s."

Today in mathematics class, your child has been solving problems like the one in the first example above—problems in which the arrow rule is given and some of the numbers in the frames are missing. In the next lesson, we will start doing problems like the one in the second example above—problems in which the numbers in the frames are given and the arrow rule is missing.

Frames and Arrows (cont.)

Family Note

Ask your child to tell you about Frames and Arrows. Then you can play Frames and Arrows with him or her. One player makes up a Frames-and-Arrows problem; the other player solves it.

Please return the second page of this Home Link to school tomorrow. Please save the first page for future reference.

SPECIAL NOTE: We are continuing to practice counting money in class, using real money. Please send 10 dimes to school for your child's tool-kit coin collection. We will start using the dimes in 2 or 3 days. As usual, please send the coins in a securely fastened envelope with your child's name printed on the outside. Thank you!

Find the missing numbers. How does the rule help you?

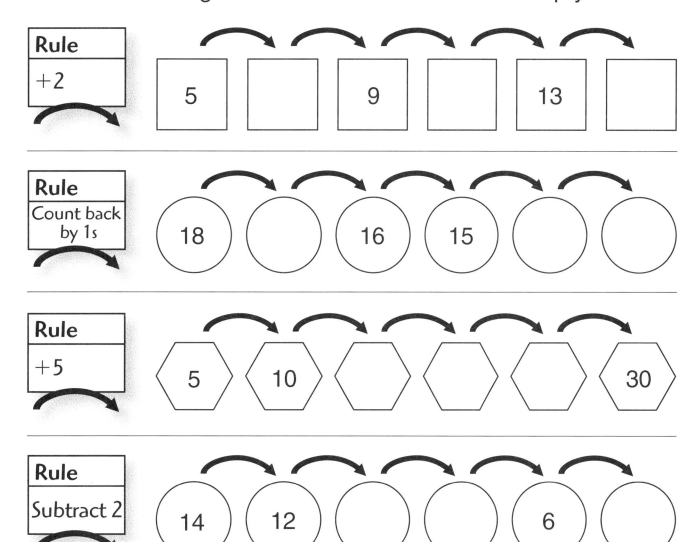

Find the Rule

Family Note

Today in mathematics class, we worked with Frames-and-Arrows diagrams in which the rule was missing. You may want to refer back to the Home Link 3.8 Family Note and review the Frames-and-Arrows routine.

Please return this Home Link to school tomorrow.

Show someone at home how to find the rules. Then find each rule.

1.

Rule

3   5   7   9   11

2.

Rule

5   10   15   20   25

3.

Rule

18   15   12   9   6

Challenge

4. Find the rule. Then fill in the missing numbers.

Rule

10   9   8   ☐   ☐   ☐

Use with Lesson 3.9.

Dimes

Family Note

Note that ⓟ means "penny," ⓝ means "nickel," and ⓓ means "dime."
    The picture on the HEADS side of a dime is of Franklin Roosevelt. On the TAILS side, there is a torch, a laurel, and an oak.

IMPORTANT: Please send 10 dimes with your child to class tomorrow.

Please return this Home Link to school tomorrow.

Look closely at a dime.

1. Who is on the HEADS side?

_____

2. What is on the TAILS side?

_____

3. How many?

_____ ⓟ = 1 ⓝ

_____ ⓝ = 1 ⓓ

_____ ⓟ = 1 ⓓ

4. How much?

ⓝ ⓝ ⓟ ⓟ ⓟ = _____ ¢

ⓟ ⓝ ⓝ ⓝ ⓟ ⓟ ⓟ = _____ ¢

ⓝ ⓝ ⓝ ⓝ ⓝ ⓝ = _____ ¢

Coin Exchanges

Family Note

First graders do not always know how to represent a given amount of money with the fewest number of coins. That's OK. At this stage, what's important is that your child understands that 5 pennies can be exchanged for 1 nickel and that 10 pennies can be exchanged for 2 nickels or 1 dime.

Please return this Home Link to school tomorrow.

1 cent 1¢ Ⓟ	5 cents 5¢ Ⓝ	10 cents 10¢ Ⓓ

1. Tell or show someone at home how many dimes you get for 4 nickels.

2. Show each amount below using the fewest coins. Use Ⓟ, Ⓝ, and Ⓓ.

(*Hint:* Exchange pennies for nickels and nickels for dimes.) Then write how much the coins are worth.

Example Ⓟ Ⓟ Ⓟ Ⓟ Ⓟ Ⓟ is the same as Ⓝ Ⓟ.

This is 6 cents.

3. Ⓟ Ⓟ Ⓟ Ⓟ Ⓟ Ⓟ Ⓟ Ⓟ Ⓟ Ⓟ is the same as _____.

This is _____ cents.

Coin Exchanges (cont.)

4. Ⓟ Ⓟ Ⓟ Ⓟ Ⓟ Ⓟ Ⓟ Ⓟ Ⓟ Ⓟ Ⓟ is the same

as _____.

This is _____ cents.

5. Ⓝ Ⓟ Ⓟ Ⓟ Ⓟ Ⓟ Ⓟ Ⓟ Ⓟ Ⓟ is the same

as _____.

This is _____ cents.

Challenge

6. Ⓝ Ⓝ Ⓝ Ⓟ Ⓟ Ⓟ Ⓟ Ⓟ Ⓟ Ⓟ Ⓟ Ⓟ is the

same as _____.

This is _____ cents.

7. Ⓝ Ⓟ Ⓝ Ⓟ Ⓝ Ⓟ Ⓟ Ⓟ is the same as _____.

This is _____ cents.

Counting Coins

Family Note

We have begun to count coin combinations consisting of pennies, nickels, and dimes. We are also starting to use dollars-and-cents notation. Help your child with the problems on this page. The Challenge problem is difficult because the coins are in no particular order. It might help to sort real coins into groups of like coins (all dimes together, all nickels together, all pennies together) before counting. If your child has trouble recording the amounts in dollars-and-cents notation, don't worry—this is a skill we will continue to work on throughout the year.

Please return this Home Link to school tomorrow.

1 cent 1¢ $0.01 Ⓟ	5 cents 5¢ $0.05 Ⓝ	10 cents 10¢ $0.10 Ⓓ

How much money? Write each answer in cents and in dollars-and-cents.

1. Ⓓ Ⓝ Ⓝ Ⓝ _____¢ *or* $_____

2. Ⓓ Ⓓ Ⓝ Ⓝ Ⓝ Ⓝ Ⓝ _____¢ *or* $_____

3. Ⓓ Ⓝ Ⓝ Ⓟ Ⓟ Ⓟ _____¢ *or* $_____

4. Ⓓ Ⓓ Ⓝ Ⓝ Ⓝ Ⓟ Ⓟ _____¢ *or* $_____

Challenge

5. Ⓟ Ⓟ Ⓝ Ⓟ Ⓓ Ⓝ Ⓝ Ⓓ Ⓝ _____¢ *or* $_____

Use with Lesson 3.12.

Favorite Colors

Family Note

Today we made a line plot for our class like the one below. At this time, your child should begin to see that the tallest column shows the color chosen by the greatest number of people and the shortest column shows the color chosen by the fewest number of people.

Please return this Home Link to school tomorrow.

1. Tell someone at home what the favorite color was in your class today.

2. In Jerry's class, children made this line plot for their favorite color.

    a. What was their **favorite** color?

    _____

    b. What was their **least favorite** color?

    _____

3. Explain to someone at home how you know the answers to these questions.

red	green	yellow	blue
			B
			B
			B
R	G		B
R	G		B
R	G		B
R	G	Y	B
R	G	Y	B
R	G	Y	B

Name   Date

Domino Top-It

Family Note

Today your child examined dot patterns on dominoes and learned a game played with dominos. The relationship between the numbers represented by the dots on each domino part and those on the entire domino is useful for work with basic facts.

Domino Top-It is a great game for helping your child practice basic addition facts.

Show someone at home how to play *Domino Top-It*. Use a set of real dominoes, if you have one. Or use the dominoes on the sheets your teacher gave you.

Directions

1. If you have real dominoes, turn them facedown on the table.

If you are using paper dominoes, put them facedown in a stack.

2. Each player turns over a domino.

If you are using paper dominoes, take one from the top of the stack.

3. The player with the larger total number of dots takes both dominoes. First estimate, then count.

In case of a tie, each player turns over another domino. The player with the larger total takes all the dominoes that are faceup.

4. The game is over when all the dominoes have been played.

The player who has more dominoes wins the game.

Use with Lesson 3.14.

Family Letter

Unit 4: Measurement and Basic Facts

Unit 4 focuses primarily on length measurement. Lesson activities will provide various opportunities for children to measure with nonstandard units, such as hand spans and paces, as well as with standard units, such as feet and inches, using a ruler and a tape measure.

Children will practice basic measuring skills, such as marking off units "end to end," aligning the 0-mark of a ruler with one edge of the object being measured, and measuring objects longer than the ruler.

Since most measurements are estimates, you will notice that the language of estimation is used when reporting measurements. For example, measurements are given as *about* 5 hand spans, *a little less than* 8 inches, *almost* 3 feet, and so on.

Copyright © SRA/McGraw-Hill

Children will also practice other measurement skills in this unit. Children will begin to read thermometers that have marks at two-degree intervals, and they will start telling time to the nearest quarter-hour. Children will also explore timelines to begin to develop a sense for the sequence of events with the passage of time.

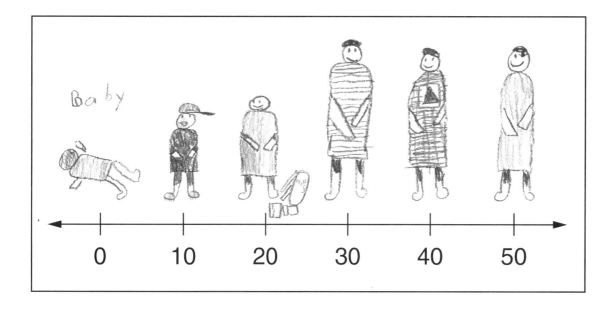

In this unit, children will begin making number scrolls by writing numbers in extended number grids. This activity not only provides practice with writing numbers, but also helps children develop a sense of the patterns in our place-value system.

−9	−8	−7	−6	−5	−4	−3	−2	−1	0
1	2	3	4	5	6	7	8	9	10
11	12	13	14	15	16	17	18	19	20
21	22	23	24	25	26	27	28	29	30
31	32	33	34	35	36	37	38	39	40
41	42	43	44	45	46	47	48	49	50
51	52	53	54	55	56	57	58	59	60
61	62	63	64	65	66	67	68	69	70
71	72	73	74	75	76	77	78	79	80
81	82	83	84	85	86	87	88	89	90
91	92	93	94	95	96	97	98	99	100

Beginning Scroll Page

In the last two lessons of the unit, children will begin working toward developing addition "fact power." Knowing the basic facts is as important to mathematics as knowing words by sight is to reading. This beginning work uses dominoes as models for the basic addition facts.

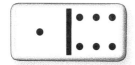

$1 + 6 = 7$

$2 + 3 = 5$

$5 + 4 = 9$

Use with Lesson 3.15.

Vocabulary

Important terms in Unit 4:

inch and foot Units of length in the U.S. customary system.

standard unit A uniform unit of measure, such as inch and foot.

timeline A device for showing in sequence when events took place.

number scroll A roll of paper with numbers written on it.

fact power Development of basic number-fact reflexes so that the facts are known without having to figure them out.

$3 + 6 = 9$

$6 + 3 = 9$

$9 - 3 = 6$

$9 - 6 = 3$

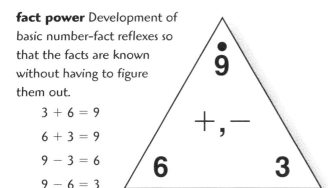

addition facts The 100 possible combinations of two one-digit numbers—from the combination with the smallest sum, $0 + 0$, to the combination with the largest sum, $9 + 9$.

+ −	0	1	2	3	4	5	6	7	8	9
0	0	1	2	3	4	5	6	7	8	9
1	1	2	3	4	5	6	7	8	9	10
2	2	3	4	5	6	7	8	9	10	11
3	3	4	5	6	7	8	9	10	11	12
4	4	5	6	7	8	9	10	11	12	13
5	5	6	7	8	9	10	11	12	13	14
6	6	7	8	9	10	11	12	13	14	15
7	7	8	9	10	11	12	13	14	15	16
8	8	9	10	11	12	13	14	15	16	17
9	9	10	11	12	13	14	15	16	17	18

As You Help Your Child with Homework

As your child brings home assignments, you may want to go over the instructions together, clarifying them as necessary. The answers listed below will guide you through this unit's Home Links.

Home Link 4.1

1. 20, 22, 24, 26, 28, 30, 32, 34, 36

2. 50, 52, 54, 56, 58, 60, 62, 64, 66

3. 70°F **4.** 60°F **5.** 80°F **6.** 58°F

7. **8.** **9.** **10.**

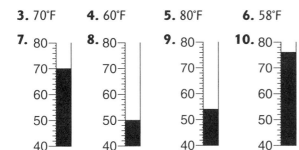

Home Link 4.7

1. 10 **2.** 12 **3.** 11

4. 9 **5.** 9 **6.** 9

Home Link 4.8

1. 1 o'clock **2.** half-past 4 o'clock

3. half-past 8 o'clock **4.** 7 o'clock

5. quarter-past 6 o'clock **6.** quarter-to 2 o'clock

Home Link 4.11

1. 6 **2.** 7 **3.** 7 **4.** 9

5. 5 **6.** 5 **7.** 6 **8.** 9

9. 7 **10.** 8 **11.** 7 **12.** 10

Use with Lesson 3.15.

Do-Anytime Activities

To work with your child on the concepts taught in this unit and in previous units, try these interesting and rewarding activities:

1 Use a standard measuring tool (such as a ruler, a tape measure, or a yardstick) to measure objects located in the house. Keep an ongoing list of items measured and their approximate lengths and widths using inches.

2 Practice counting by 2s using a thermometer.

3 Tell the time (on the hour, the half-hour, or the quarter-hour) and have your child draw a picture of a clock representing that time.

4 Have your child tell you the time as minutes after the hour. *For example:* "It is about six-fifteen" or "It is about fifteen minutes after six."

5 Have your child tell you a number story that goes with a given number sentence, such as 3 + 5 = 8. *For example:* "I had 3 dogs. Then I got 5 more dogs. Now I have 8 dogs!"

Reading Thermometers

Family Note

Children are beginning to read thermometers marked in two-degree intervals. A skill that you can easily practice with your child at home, which will help with reading temperatures, is to count by 2s. Begin with multiples of 10 (numbers like 10, 20, 30, and so on). For example, start at 50 and count by 2s: 50, 52, 54, 56, 58, 60, and so on.

Please return this Home Link to school tomorrow.

Fill in the frames.

1.

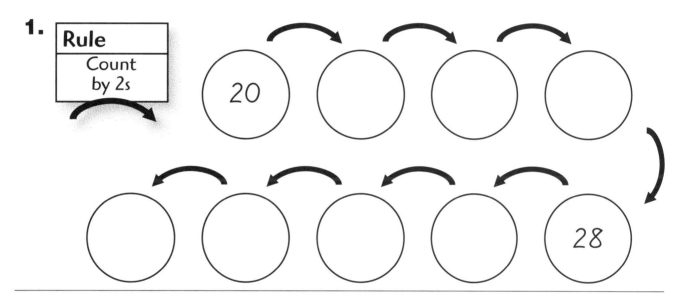

Rule — Count by 2s

20   ○   ○   ○

○   ○   ○   ○   28

2.

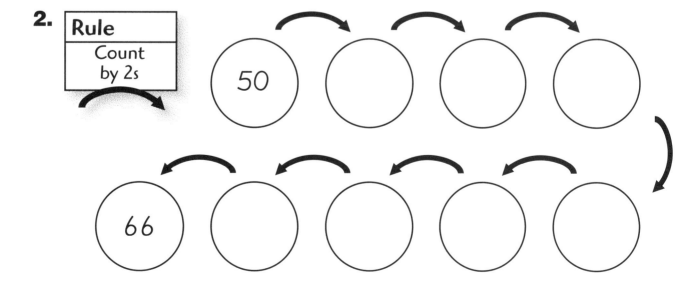

Rule — Count by 2s

50   ○   ○   ○

66   ○   ○   ○   ○

Thermometers (cont.)

Write the temperature shown by each thermometer.
Write °F with the temperature.

Challenge

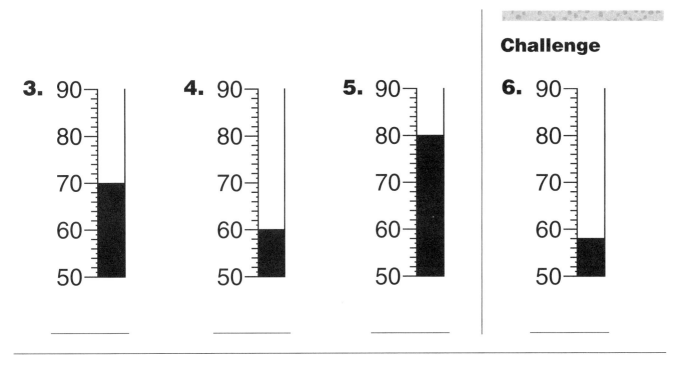

3.   **4.**   **5.**   **6.**

Color the mercury to show each temperature.

Challenge

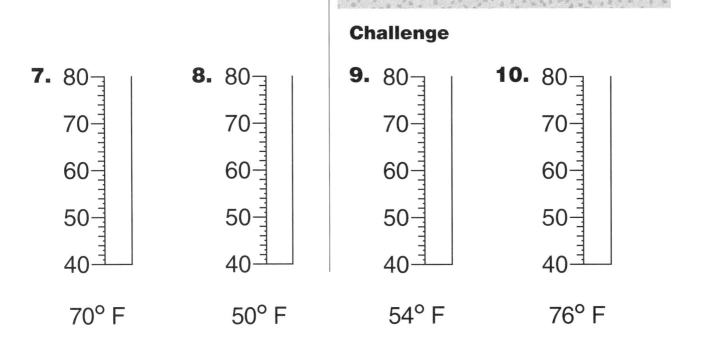

7. 70° F   **8.** 50° F   **9.** 54° F   **10.** 76° F

           Use with Lesson 4.1.

Measuring with Hand Spans

Family Note

In today's lesson, we measured objects using nonstandard units like digits (finger widths), hands, fathoms, and hand spans.

One of our discoveries is that we get different measurements for the same object if different people do the measuring using these units. We will continue this investigation, eventually realizing that standard units, such as feet and inches, provide us with more reliable measurements. Help your child measure his or her bed using hand spans. The drawing below shows a hand span.

Please return this Home Link to school tomorrow.

Measure your bed with your hand span.

1. How many hand spans across is it?

About _____ hand spans

2. How many hand spans long is it?

About _____ hand spans

3. Draw a picture of your bed.

The Foot-Long Foot

Family Note

To help us investigate the measuring unit "feet," please help your child trace each family member's foot using different-color crayons.

Please return this Home Link to school tomorrow.

Compare the foot-long foot to the feet of members of your family.

Here is what you do:

1. Trace each person's foot onto the foot-long foot. Use a different-color crayon for each person's foot.

2. Label each traced foot with the person's name.

3. Talk about why it is not a good idea for people to use their own feet for measuring things.

Use with Lesson 4.3.

Measuring with Inches

Family Note

We are just beginning to measure to the nearest inch. Do not expect your child to be proficient with this skill at this time. We will be practicing throughout the year. To help your child, make sure that he or she lines up one end of the object being measured with the "0-mark" on the ruler. Help your child find the closest inch mark at the other end of the object. (We have used the $\frac{1}{2}$ inch marks to find the closest inch marks).

Please return this Home Link to school tomorrow.

Cut out the ruler at the bottom of this page. Use it to measure four small objects. Draw a picture of each object. Write the measurements.

1.

About _____ inches long

2.

About _____ inches long

3.

About _____ inches long

4.

About _____ inches long

```
0   INCHES   1       2       3       4       5       6
```

Name _____   Date _____

Family Note

This activity is the same as the activity on the previous Home Link, except that this ruler is marked in sixteenths of an inch. Although the marks for fractions of an inch may distract your child, this ruler is the same as the tool-kit ruler we use at school. Your child may find that it helps to "color" the inch marks.

Have your child measure objects to the nearest inch. Make sure your child lines up one end of the object being measured with the "0-mark" on the ruler.

Please return this Home Link to school tomorrow.

Cut out the ruler at the bottom of this page. Use it to measure four small objects to the nearest inch. Draw a picture of each object. Record your measurements.

1.

About _____ inches long

2.

About _____ inches long

3.

About _____ inches long

4.

About _____ inches long

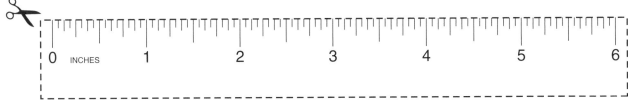

Use with Lesson 4.5.

Measuring Tools

Family Note

In class, we have been working with linear measures, using rulers and tape measures. The length of an object is an example of a linear measure.

Help your child find rulers and tape measures in your home. You and your child may also include other kinds of measuring tools, such as scales that measure weight, measuring cups that measure capacity, and so on.

Please return this Home Link to school tomorrow.

Name and draw 3 measuring tools in your home.

Example

1.

2.

3.

Domino Dots

Family Note

Dominoes are a great way to develop readiness for addition and subtraction facts. We will do a lot of work with dominoes this year.

Please return this Home Link to school tomorrow.

Draw the missing dots on each domino.
Write the total number of dots.

1. _____
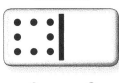
8   2

2. _____
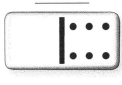
6   6

3. _____
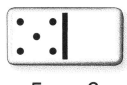
5   6

4. _____
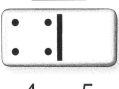
4   5

5. _____

7   2

6. _____
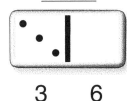
3   6

Challenge

Draw missing dots on each domino.
Write the numbers for each set of dots and for the total.

7. _____
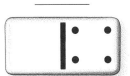
_____   _____

8. _____
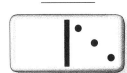
_____   _____

Make up
your own.

9. _____

_____   _____

Use with Lesson 4.7.

Telling Time

Family Note

Before today, we have been learning to tell time on the hour and the half-hour. Today we began to learn how to tell time on the quarter-hour.

Please return this Home Link to school tomorrow.

Record the time.

1.

_____ o'clock

2.

half-past

_____ o'clock

3.

half-past

_____ o'clock

4.

_____ o'clock

Challenge

5.

quarter-past

_____ o'clock

6.

quarter-to

_____ o'clock

Use with Lesson 4.8.

Write the years below. Then on the back of this page, draw pictures of important things that happened in your family each year since you were born.

My 8th birthday

My 7th birthday

My 6th birthday

My 5th birthday

My 4th birthday

My 3rd birthday

My 2nd birthday

My 1st birthday

I was born.

Number Grids

Family Note

Ordering numbers in a grid is important in identifying number patterns and developing number power. You and your child may want to talk about any patterns in the section of a number grid shown below.

Please return this Home Link to school tomorrow.

1. Tell your family how you filled in number grids and made scrolls.

2. Ask if your family knows about any other kinds of scrolls.

3. Show someone how you can fill in the bottom 3 rows of this number grid.

									100
101									
				115					
									130

Review

How much money? Write each answer in cents and dollars-and-cents.

4. Ⓓ Ⓝ Ⓝ Ⓟ Ⓟ Ⓟ _____ ¢ or $_____

5. Ⓓ Ⓓ Ⓓ Ⓝ Ⓝ Ⓟ _____ ¢ or $_____

Family Note

We have started our work with basic addition facts. The basic facts include sums for the facts from $0 + 0$ through $9 + 9$. At this beginning stage, your child may still need to count the total number of dots on the dominoes to complete the problems.

Please return this Home Link to school tomorrow.

Find the sums.

1.
$$\begin{array}{r} 4 \\ + 2 \\ \hline \end{array}$$

2.
$$\begin{array}{r} 6 \\ + 1 \\ \hline \end{array}$$

3.
$$\begin{array}{r} 7 \\ + 0 \\ \hline \end{array}$$

4.
$$\begin{array}{r} 8 \\ + 1 \\ \hline \end{array}$$

5.

$1 + 4 = \underline{\hspace{1cm}}$

6.

$\underline{\hspace{1cm}} = 2 + 3$

7.

$3 + 3 = \underline{\hspace{1cm}}$

8.

$\underline{\hspace{1cm}} = 0 + 9$

9.
$$\begin{array}{r} 3 \\ + 4 \\ \hline \end{array}$$

10.
$$\begin{array}{r} 2 \\ + 6 \\ \hline \end{array}$$

11.
$$\begin{array}{r} 5 \\ + 2 \\ \hline \end{array}$$

12.
$$\begin{array}{r} 8 \\ + 2 \\ \hline \end{array}$$

Challenge

13. Draw a domino of your choice.
Write a fact to go with it.

   _____

Use with Lesson 4.11.

Color-by-Number

Family Note

We are continuing our work with addition facts. Now we are working with facts using +0, +1, +2 (such as 3 + 0, 5 + 1, and 8 + 2) and doubles facts (such as 2 + 2 and 4 + 4).

Please return this Home Link to school tomorrow.

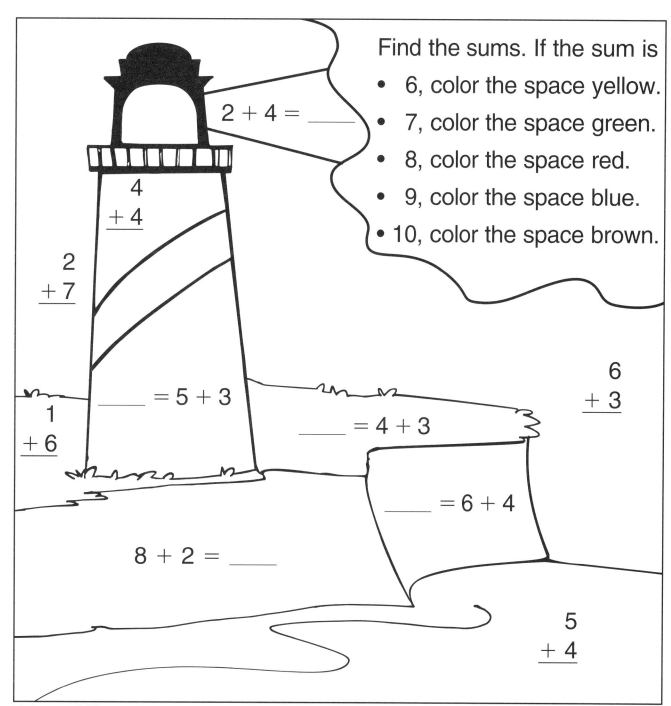

Find the sums. If the sum is

- 6, color the space yellow.
- 7, color the space green.
- 8, color the space red.
- 9, color the space blue.
- 10, color the space brown.

$2 + 4 =$ _____

$\begin{array}{r} 4 \\ + 4 \\ \hline \end{array}$

$\begin{array}{r} 2 \\ + 7 \\ \hline \end{array}$

_____ $= 5 + 3$

$\begin{array}{r} 1 \\ + 6 \\ \hline \end{array}$

_____ $= 4 + 3$

$\begin{array}{r} 6 \\ + 3 \\ \hline \end{array}$

_____ $= 6 + 4$

$8 + 2 =$ _____

$\begin{array}{r} 5 \\ + 4 \\ \hline \end{array}$

Unit 5: Place Value, Number Stories, and Basic Facts

As their work in mathematics progresses, children are beginning to use larger numbers. In Unit 5, children will begin to explore the system we use for writing large numbers by focusing on the idea of **place value.** For example, in the number 72, 7 is in the tens place, so there are "7 tens," and 2 is in the ones place, so there are "2 ones." Children will use base-10 blocks to represent numbers and to find the sums of two numbers. They will also use place value to determine "greater than" and "less than" relationships.

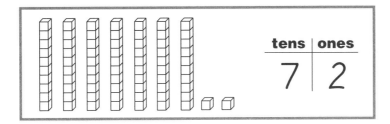

Later in this unit, children will continue to work with addition facts. Shortcuts for learning facts will be introduced. One shortcut is the **turn-around rule,** which states that the order in which numbers are added does not change the sum. For example, 4 + 3 and 3 + 4 both equal 7. Your child will also learn the meaning of adding 0 and 1 to any number. Knowing these shortcuts will make the task of learning addition facts easier.

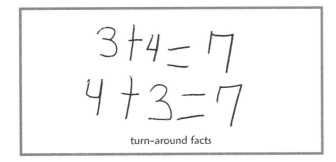

turn-around facts

Children will also practice place value and addition and subtraction facts by acting out number stories. They will act out these stories using concrete objects and begin to represent the stories with **number models.** (See this unit's vocabulary list for more information on number models.)

Children have explored many number patterns in previous lessons. **"What's My Rule?"** is a routine introduced in this unit and found throughout *Everyday Mathematics* that provides practice with number patterns and number relationships. You will receive more detailed information about this routine when we begin to use it in class.

Please keep this Family Letter for reference as your child works through Unit 5.

Vocabulary

Important terms in Unit 5:

cube A base-10 block that represents 1.

long A base-10 block that represents 10.

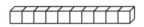

flat A base-10 block that represents 100.

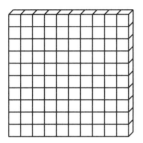

place value The quantity a digit represents in a number. This quantity, or value, is determined by the digit's position in the number. For example, in the number 52, the 5 represents 5 tens, and the 2 represents 2 ones.

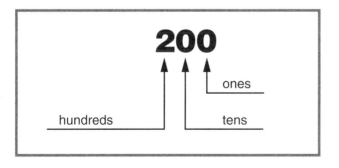

number model A numerical representation that shows how the parts of a number story are related.

Example of a number story:

Seven lions are lying in the sun. Three more lions join them. How many lions are there altogether?

Example of a number model:

$7 + 3 = 10$

Unit
lions

turn-around addition facts Two addition facts in which the same two numbers are being added, but they appear in a different order. For example, $5 + 4 = 9$ and $4 + 5 = 9$ are turn-around addition facts.

doubles fact An addition fact in which both numbers being added are the same. For example, $5 + 5 = 10$; $2 + 2 = 4$; and $6 + 6 = 12$ are all doubles facts.

function machine A diagram of an imaginary machine programmed to process numbers according to a certain rule. A number (input) is put into the machine and is transformed into a second number (output) through the application of a rule.

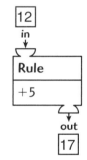

"What's My Rule?" A routine that consists of a set of number pairs in which the numbers in each pair are related to each other according to the same rule. The problems are usually displayed in table format, in which two of the three parts are known. The goal is to find the unknown part.

Rule
+5

in	out
2	7
5	10
7	12
6	11

Do-Anytime Activities

To work with your child on the concepts taught in this unit and in previous units, try these interesting and rewarding activities:

1 Tell addition and subtraction number stories. Have your child solve the problems using various household objects and then record the answers in number models. Remember to give a context for the numbers, such as coins, animals, types of clothing, and so on.

2 Encourage your child to make up some number stories, too.

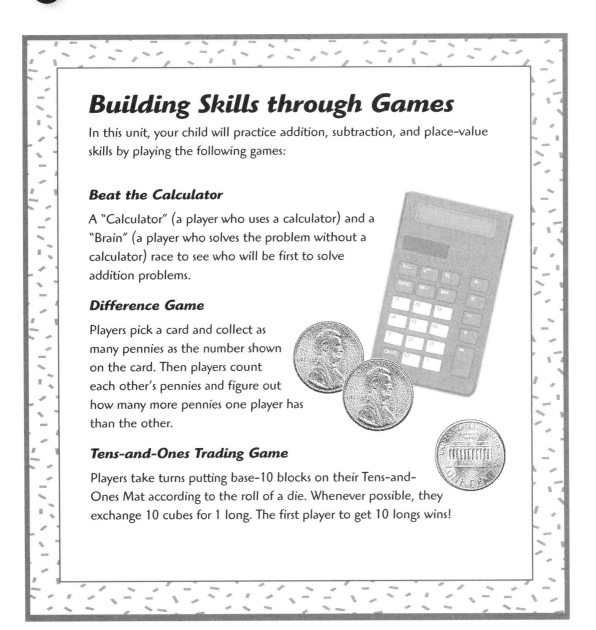

Building Skills through Games

In this unit, your child will practice addition, subtraction, and place-value skills by playing the following games:

Beat the Calculator

A "Calculator" (a player who uses a calculator) and a "Brain" (a player who solves the problem without a calculator) race to see who will be first to solve addition problems.

Difference Game

Players pick a card and collect as many pennies as the number shown on the card. Then players count each other's pennies and figure out how many more pennies one player has than the other.

Tens-and-Ones Trading Game

Players take turns putting base-10 blocks on their Tens-and-Ones Mat according to the roll of a die. Whenever possible, they exchange 10 cubes for 1 long. The first player to get 10 longs wins!

Use with Lesson 4.13.

As You Help Your Child with Homework

As your child brings home assignments, you may want to go over the instructions together, clarifying them as necessary. The answers listed below will guide you through this unit's Home Links.

Home Link 5.1

1. 56 **2.** 73 **3.** 12 **4.** 49

Home Link 5.2

1. 20, 30, 40, 50, 60, 70

2. 120, 110, 100, 90, 80, 70

3. 88, 78, 68, 58, 48, 38

4. 4, 14, 24, 34, 44, 54

Home Link 5.3

1. > **2.** < **3.** = **4.** <

5. > **6.** < **7.** > **8.** =

Home Link 5.4

1. 32¢, or $0.32 **2.** 36¢, or $0.36

3. 38¢, or $0.38 **4.** 50¢, or $0.50

Home Link 5.5

1. 8 **2.** 12 **3.** 4

4. 6 **5.** 3 **6.** 6

7. 6 **8.** 9 **9.** 4

10.

$$\begin{array}{r} 8 \\ + 8 \\ \hline 16 \end{array}$$

11.

$$5 + \underline{\quad 5 \quad} = 10$$

Home Link 5.6

1. < **2.** > **3.** =

4. < **5.** < **6.** <

Home Link 5.7

1. Bart; 4¢ **2.** Martha; 7¢

3. Maria; 8¢ **4.** Michelle; 11¢

Home Link 5.9

1. > **2.** < **3.** =

4. = **5.** =

Home Link 5.10

1. 6 + 3 = 9 **2.** 3 + 6 = 9

3. 5 + 4 = 9 **4.** 4 + 5 = 9

Home Link 5.12

1. Rule +1

in	out
6	7
14	15
26	27
19	20
9	10

Your turn:

2. Rule −2

in	out
10	8
22	20
25	23
12	10
21	19

Your turn:

3. Rule +10

in	out
36	46
19	29
62	72
25	35

Your turn:

4. Rule half of

in	out
2	1
4	2
6	3
8	4

Your turn:

Home Link 5.13

1. Rule +3

2. Rule −10

in	out
13	3
26	16
45	35

4. Rule +2

in	out
3	5
1	3
0	2

Name _____ Date _____

Tens-and-Ones Riddles

Family Note

We have begun to work on place value using base-10 blocks. The blocks shown in the tens columns are called *longs* and the blocks shown in the ones columns are called *cubes*. It takes 10 cubes to make 1 long. On this page, your child is writing the numbers shown with longs and cubes. The Challenge problem is difficult because you need to exchange 10 of the cubes for 1 long before you can write the number. If your child has trouble with this problem, you might use dimes for the longs and pennies for the cubes and exchange 10 pennies for a dime.

Please return this Home Link to school tomorrow.

Example

Tens	Ones

What number am I? __28__

1.

Tens	Ones

What number am I? _____

2.

Tens	Ones

What number am I? _____

3.

Tens	Ones

What number am I? _____

Challenge

4.

Tens	Ones

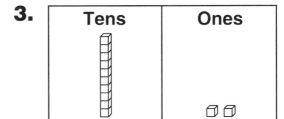

What number am I? _____

Use with Lesson 5.1.

Name _____   Date _____

Frames-and-Arrows Diagrams

Family Note

Children continue to work with place value and base-10 blocks. One of the activities in this lesson was to count up and back by 10s from any number. On this page, your child will continue to explore what happens to the digits in a numeral when counting by 10s. Note that the Challenge problem may be difficult for your child because it requires working backward to complete the first frame.

Please return this Home Link to school tomorrow.

Find the missing numbers in these diagrams.

1.

Rule
$+10$

20 ☐ ☐ ☐ 60 ☐

2.

Rule
-10

120 ☐ ☐ ☐ 80 ☐

3.

Rule
Count back by 10s

88 ☐ ☐ 58 ☐ ☐

Challenge

4.

Rule
Add 10

☐ 14 ☐ ☐ 44 ☐

Relation Symbols

Family Note

The relation symbols < and > were introduced in this lesson. The symbol < means *is less than* and the symbol > means *is greater than*. These symbols will be used from now on in the same way we use the symbol = for *is equal to* or *equals*. For example, instead of writing 5 *is less than* 8, we will write 5 < 8.

It takes time for children to learn the correct use of these symbols. One way to help your child identify the correct symbol is to draw two dots near the larger number and one dot near the smaller number. Then connect each of the two dots to the single dot.

$$5 < 8$$

Another way is to think of the open end of the symbol as a mouth swallowing the larger number.

Write <, >, or =.

Example

18 __>__ 12

< is less than
> is more than
= is the same as
= is equal to

1. 11 _____ 7   **2.** 21 _____ 25   **3.** 37 _____ 37

4. 29 _____ 42   **5.** 35 _____ 15   **6.** 48 _____ 128

Challenge

7. 16 _____ 5 + 10   **8.** 8 + 2 _____ 10

Counting Coins

Family Note

Children are continuing to practice counting coins. The Challenge problem is difficult because the coins are not in any particular order. It might help to sort real coins into groups of like coins (all dimes together, all nickels together) before counting. To find a combination with fewer coins, exchange pennies for nickels and nickels for dimes. Many children are still learning to write amounts of money using dollars-and-cents notation. We will continue to practice this skill during the year.

Please return this Home Link to school tomorrow.

(P) 1 cent	(N) 5 cents	(D) 10 cents
$0.01	$0.05	$0.10
a penny	a nickel	a dime

How much? Write each answer in cents and in dollars-and-cents notation.

1. (D)(N)(N)(N)(N)(P)(P) _____¢ or $____.____

2. (D)(N)(N)(N)(N)(N)(P) _____¢ or $____.____

3. (D)(D)(N)(N)(N)(P)(P)(P) _____¢ or $____.____

Challenge

4. (P)(P)(N)(P)(D)(D)(N)(D)(N)(P)(P) _____¢ or $____.____

On the back of this paper show this amount with fewer coins. Use (P), (N), and (D).

Domino Addition

Family Note

Children are continuing to practice basic addition facts. Notice that we are emphasizing +0, +1, +2, and double facts like 3 + 3.

Please return this Home Link to school tomorrow.

Add.

1. 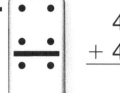 $\begin{array}{r} 4 \\ + 4 \\ \hline \end{array}$

2.  $\begin{array}{r} 6 \\ + 6 \\ \hline \end{array}$

3.  $\begin{array}{r} 2 \\ + 2 \\ \hline \end{array}$

4.  $\begin{array}{r} 0 \\ + 6 \\ \hline \end{array}$

5.

___ = 2 + 1

6.

1 + 5 = ___

7.

3 + 3 = ___

8.

___ = 0 + 9

Fill in the missing dots and fill in the missing numbers.

9.  $\begin{array}{r} 4 \\ + 0 \\ \hline \end{array}$

10. 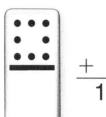 $\begin{array}{r} 8 \\ + \\ \hline 16 \end{array}$

11.

5 + ___ = 10

Challenge

12. Draw a domino of your choice.
Write an addition fact to go with it.

_____

Use with Lesson 5.5.

Name _____ Date _____

Relation Symbols

Family Note

As children continue their work with relation symbols, you can help at home by having your child read aloud the number models on this page. Read the example as follows: 65 is less than 83.

Please return this Home Link to school tomorrow.

Write <, >, or =.

Example 65 __<__ 83

> < is less than
> > is more than
> = is the same as
> = is equal to

1. 15 _____ 17

2. 28 _____ 19

3. 24 _____ 24

4. 36 _____ 63

5. 72 _____ 92

6. 55 _____ 128

Challenge

Fill in numbers to make these correct.

7. 46 < _____

8. _____ > 155

Comparing Amounts of Money

Family Note

Children are beginning to work with number stories in which they find how much more (or less) one number is than another. This is called the *difference* between the two numbers. Notice that the smaller numbers in the problems are always shown in smaller frames.

Help your child line up the pennies in two rows and pair pennies in the top row with pennies in the bottom row. Have your child make as many pairs as possible. The extra pennies that could not be paired off represent the difference.

Please return this Home Link to school tomorrow.

1. Bart ⓟⓟⓟⓟⓟⓟⓟⓟⓟⓟⓟⓟ

Perry ⓟⓟⓟⓟⓟⓟⓟⓟ

Who has more? _____ How much more? _____ ¢

2. Tricia ⓟⓟⓟ

Martha ⓟⓟⓟⓟⓟⓟⓟⓟⓟ

Who has more? _____ How much more? _____ ¢

3. Franklin | 17 pennies |

Maria | 25 pennies |

Who has more? _____ How much more? _____ ¢

4. Michelle | 19 pennies |

Lawrence | 8 pennies |

Who has more? _____ How much more? _____ ¢

Number Stories

**Family
Note**

Children have been telling and solving number stories in class. Have your child explain the number story that goes with the picture he or she chooses. If you like, help your child record the number story in words. The number model may show addition or subtraction, depending on how your child tells the story.

Please return this Home Link to school tomorrow.

Here is a number story Mandy made up.

I have 4 balloons.
Jamal brought 1 more.
We have 5 balloons together.

4 + 1 = 5

Unit
balloons

Find a picture in a magazine. Use it to write a number story or draw your own picture.

Write a number model to go with your story.

Unit

Comparing Sums

Family Note

For the next few days, children will return to the basic addition facts. They will concentrate on memorizing the +1 and + 0 facts (for example, 7 + 0 and 8 + 1), doubles facts (doubles like 3 + 3), and facts that have a sum of 10 (for example, 3 + 7 and 6 + 4). This will take time and practice. Consider spending a little bit of time each day practicing these addition facts with your child.

Please return this Home Link to school tomorrow.

Write <, >, or =.

1. [3] + [5] ____ [1] + [4]

2. [1] + [6] ____ [4] + [4]

3. [3] + [3] ____ [5] + [1]

4.

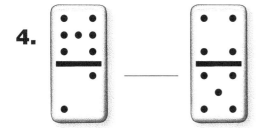

Challenge

5.

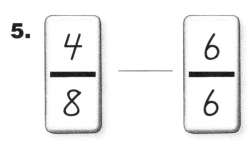

Use with Lesson 5.9.

Turn-Around Dice

Family Note

Turn-around addition facts are pairs of facts in which the numbers that are being added are the same. Turn-around facts have the same sum. For example, 2 + 3 = 5 and 3 + 2 = 5 are turn-around facts. Knowing about turn-around facts cuts down on the number of facts that have to be memorized: If you know a fact, you also know its turn-around fact.

Please return this Home Link to school tomorrow.

Find the total number of dots on the dice.
Watch for turn-around facts.

Unit
dice dots

1.

_____ + _____ = _____

2.

_____ + _____ = _____

3.

4.

Make up your own turn-around facts. Draw the dots and write the addition facts.

5. [ ] + [ ]

_____ + _____ = _____

6. [ ] + [ ]

_____ + _____ = _____

Name _____   Date _____

Adding 0 and 1

Home Link
5.11

Family Note

Give your child several 1-digit, 2-digit, and 3-digit numbers. Ask him or her to add 0 and 1 to each.

Use some numbers with 9 in the ones place like 9, 49, 79, 129, 359, and 789. Also use 0 in the tens and ones places, like in 208 and 320.

Please return this Home Link to school tomorrow.

1. Ask someone at home to say a 1-digit number; for example, 7. Add 0 to the number and give the answer. Then add 1 to the number and give the answer.

2. Have someone say a 2-digit or 3-digit number. Add 0 and 1 to this number.

3. Find the answers to more +0 and +1 problems with 2-digit or 3-digit numbers. Write them in the table below.

Example   25   25 + 0 = 25
                + 1
             ————
              26

Number Models

	Number	**+0**	**+1**
Example	25	25 + 0 = 25	25 + 1 = 26
1-digit number			
2-digit number			
3-digit number			
Your choice			

Use with Lesson 5.11.

Family Letter

"What's My Rule?"

Today your child learned about a kind of problem you may not have seen before. We call it "What's My Rule?" Please ask your child to explain it to you.

Here is a little background information you may find useful. Imagine a machine with a funnel at the top and a tube at the bottom—we call this a *function machine.* The function machine can be programmed so that if you drop a number into the funnel at the top, the machine does something to the number according to a rule to make a new number come out of the tube at the bottom. For example, you can program the machine to add 2 to any number that is dropped into the funnel. If you put in 3, out comes 5; if you put in 6, out comes 8.

You can show this with a table:

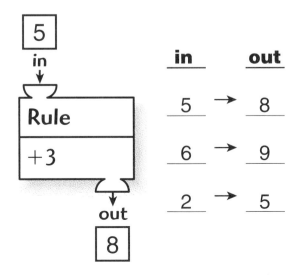

in		out
3	→	5
6	→	8
10	→	12

Here is another example of a function machine:

in		out
5	→	8
6	→	9
2	→	5

In a "What's My Rule?" problem, some of the information is missing. To solve the problem, you have to find the missing information. The missing information can be the numbers that come out, the numbers that are dropped in, or the rule for programming the machine. *For example:*

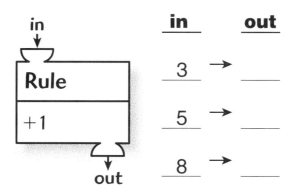

Missing "out" numbers

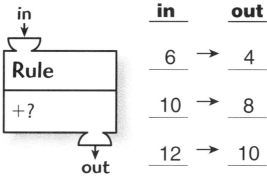

Missing rule

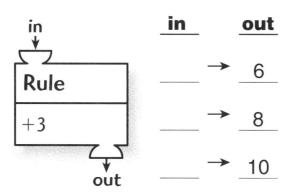

Missing "in" numbers

Use with Lesson 5.12.

"What's My Rule?"

Family Note

Ask your child to explain what the function machine is doing to the "in" numbers before filling in the missing "out" numbers. For example, in the first problem, the function machine is adding 1 to each of the "in" numbers.

The Challenge problem may prove difficult because it does not involve addition or subtraction. However, children often have an intuitive grasp of "$\frac{1}{2}$ of a number." We will continue to provide experiences with number patterns (as well as other kinds of patterns) in future lessons.

Please return this Home Link to school tomorrow.

Fill in the missing numbers.

1.

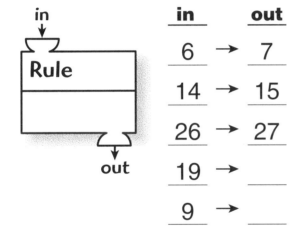

in		out
6	→	7
14	→	15
26	→	27
19	→	
9	→	

Your turn: ____ → ____

2.

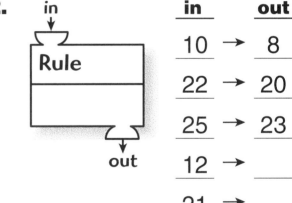

in		out
10	→	8
22	→	20
25	→	23
12	→	
21	→	

Your turn: ____ → ____

3.

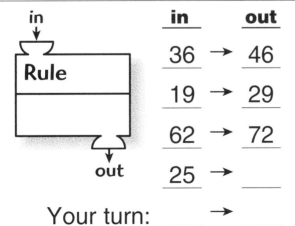

in		out
36	→	46
19	→	29
62	→	72
25	→	

Your turn: ____ → ____

Challenge

4.

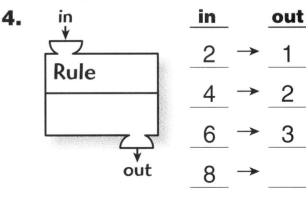

in		out
2	→	1
4	→	2
6	→	3
8	→	

Your turn: ____ → ____

Name _____   Date _____

Family Note

Children are continuing their exploration of number patterns. Each problem on this page represents a different kind of problem.

In the first problem, your child tries to find the rule.

In the second and fourth problems, the rule is given. The second problem calls for applying the rule to find the "out" numbers; the fourth problem calls for applying the rule to find the "in" numbers. This problem is especially challenging because you must do the opposite of the rule to find the "in" numbers (subtract 2).

Encourage your child to describe how he or she solved each problem.

Please return this Home Link to school tomorrow.

1. Find the rule.

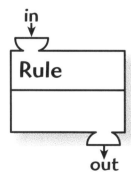

in	out
5	8
10	13
18	21

Your turn: ___

2. What comes out?

Rule −10

in	out
13	3
26	
45	

Your turn: ___

3. Make your own.

Rule

in	out

Challenge

4. What goes in?

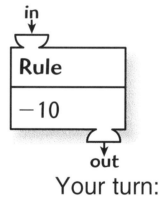

Rule +2

in	out
	5
	3
	2

Your turn: ___

Use with Lesson 5.13.

Family Letter

Unit 6: Developing Fact Power

Knowing the basic facts is as important to mathematics as knowing words by sight is to reading. Your child should start to get a good handle on many addition and subtraction facts by the end of the year.

Learning the facts takes practice. It is not necessary to practice for a long time, but it is important to practice often, almost every day. One good way to practice is to play the games that are introduced at school. (See the third page of this letter.)

In Unit 6, children will learn shortcuts that will make it easier to learn the facts. One shortcut is the turn-around rule, which simply states that the order in which numbers are added does not change the sum. For example, 3 + 4 and 4 + 3 both equal 7, so when your child has learned one of these facts, he or she automatically knows its turn-around fact. Your child will also learn how easy it is to add 0 and 1 to any number. Working with shortcuts like these will help build "fact power."

Also, children will broaden their money skills by counting coins that include quarters.

Later in this unit, children will extend their time-telling skills by learning to tell time to the nearest 5 minutes and by representing the time in digital notation, as it appears on a digital clock.

Please keep this letter for reference as your child works through Unit 6.

Use with Lesson 5.14.

Math Tools

Your child will be using **Fact Triangles** to practice and review addition and subtraction facts. Fact Triangles are a "new and improved" version of flash cards; the addition and subtraction facts shown are made from the same three numbers, and this helps your child understand the relationships among those facts. The *Family Note* on Home Link 6.4, which you will receive later, provides a more detailed description of Fact Triangles.

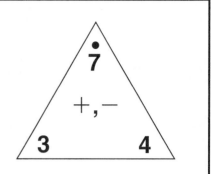

Vocabulary

Important terms in Unit 6:

addition and subtraction facts The addition facts are the 100 possible combinations of two one-digit addends. The subtraction facts are the inverses of the addition facts.

fact family A group of addition facts together with the subtraction facts. For example, the following facts form the fact family for the numbers 3, 4, and 7:

$$3 + 4 = 7$$
$$4 + 3 = 7$$
$$7 - 3 = 4$$
$$7 - 4 = 3$$

function machine A diagram of an imaginary machine programmed to process numbers according to a certain rule. A number (input) is put into the machine and is transformed into a second number (output) through the application of a rule.

name-collection box A boxlike diagram tagged with a given number and used for collecting equivalent names for that number.

digital clock A clock that uses only numbers to show the time in hours and minutes, with a colon used to separate them.

range The difference between the greatest and least numbers in a set of data. For example, in the set of data below, the difference between 36 and 28 is 8, so 8 is the range.

middle value The number in the middle when a set of data is organized in sequential order. For example, in the following set of data, 32 is the middle value:

28 28 31 32 33 35 36

"What's My Rule?" A routine that consists of a set of number pairs in which the numbers in each pair are related to each other according to the same rule. The problems are usually displayed in a table format, in which two of the three parts are known. The goal is to find the unknown part.

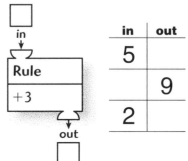

Building Skills through Games

In Unit 6, your child will practice addition, subtraction, and place-value skills by playing the following games.

Beat the Calculator

A "Calculator" (a player who uses a calculator) and a "Brain" (a player who solves the problem without a calculator) race to see who will be first to solve addition problems.

Difference Game

Players pick a card and collect as many pennies as the number shown on the card. Then players count each other's pennies and figure out how many more pennies one player has than the other.

Tens-and-Ones Trading Game

Players take turns putting base-10 blocks on their Tens-and-Ones Mat according to the roll of a die. Whenever possible, they exchange 10 cubes for 1 long. The first player to get to 10 longs wins!

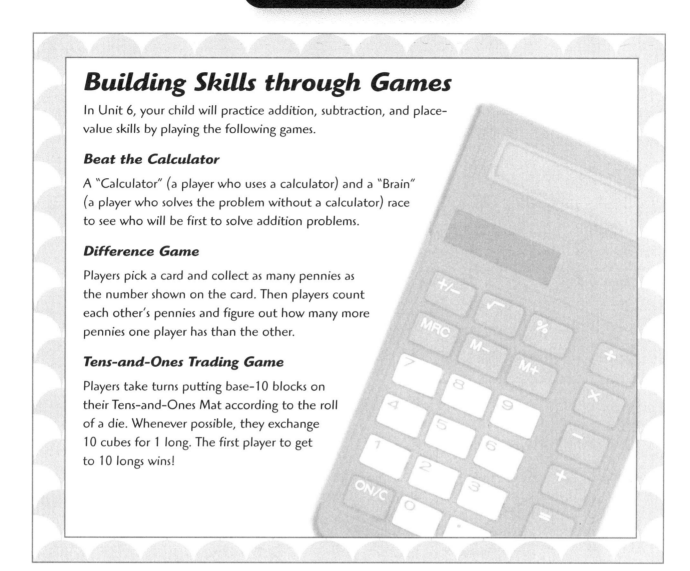

Do-Anytime Activities

To work with your child on the concepts taught in this unit and in previous units, try these interesting and rewarding activities:

1 Using the Fact Triangles, cover the sum for addition practice. Cover one of the other numbers for subtraction practice. Make this brief and fun.

2 Have your child tell you a number story that fits a given number model, such as $3 + 5 = 8$.

3 Go to your local library and check out the book *12 Ways to Get to 11* by Eve Merriam, an entertaining book that presents addition facts.

4 Play with name-collection boxes. Begin with a number, such as 20, and find at least five equivalent names for the number.

Use with Lesson 5.14.

As You Help Your Child with Homework

As your child brings home assignments, you may want to go over the instructions together, clarifying them as necessary. The answers listed below will guide you through this unit's Home Links.

Home Link 6.3

1. 5, 7, 12; 5 + 7 = 12; 7 + 5 = 12;
12 − 5 = 7; 12 − 7 = 5

2. 6, 9, 15; 6 + 9 = 15; 9 + 6 = 15;
15 − 6 = 9; 15 − 9 = 6

3. 8, 8, 16; 8 + 8 = 16; 16 − 8 = 8

Home Link 6.5

1. 3, 9, 12; 3 + 9 = 12; 9 + 3 = 12;
12 − 3 = 9; 12 − 9 = 3

3.

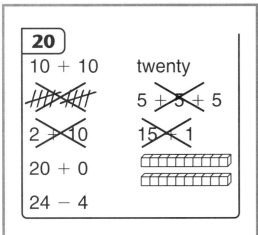

Home Link 6.8

3. George Washington; 25 (P); 25¢; 5 (N)

Home Link 6.9

1. 50¢, or $0.50

2. 82¢, or $0.82

3. 43¢, or $0.43

4. 72¢, or $0.72

5. 121¢, or $1.21

Home Link 6.10

1.

2.

3.

Home Link 6.12

1. 25

2. 18

3. 5

4. 13

Use with Lesson 5.14.

Using the Addition Table

Family Note

Children are continuing to practice addition facts in class. Today they learned how to use the facts table to help find sums. Children used sheets of paper and lined them up as illustrated at the right.

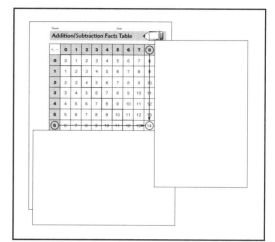

+, −	0	1	2	3	4	5	6	7	8	9
0	0	1	2	3	4	5	6	7	8	9
1	1	2	3	4	5	6	7	8	9	10
2	2	3	4	5	6	7	8	9	10	11
3	3	4	5	6	7	8	9	10	11	12
4	4	5	6	7	8	9	10	11	12	13
5	5	6	7	8	9	10	11	12	13	14
6	6	7	8	9	10	11	12	13	14	15
7	7	8	9	10	11	12	13	14	15	16
8	8	9	10	11	12	13	14	15	16	17
9	9	10	11	12	13	14	15	16	17	18

Help your child find sums in the table. It is OK to solve the problems using other strategies, such as counting on or using counters to model the problems.

Please return this Home Link to school tomorrow.

Using the Addition Table (cont.)

Use the color code to color the picture.

Color Code

10 = green   14 = yellow
12 = blue   15 = red

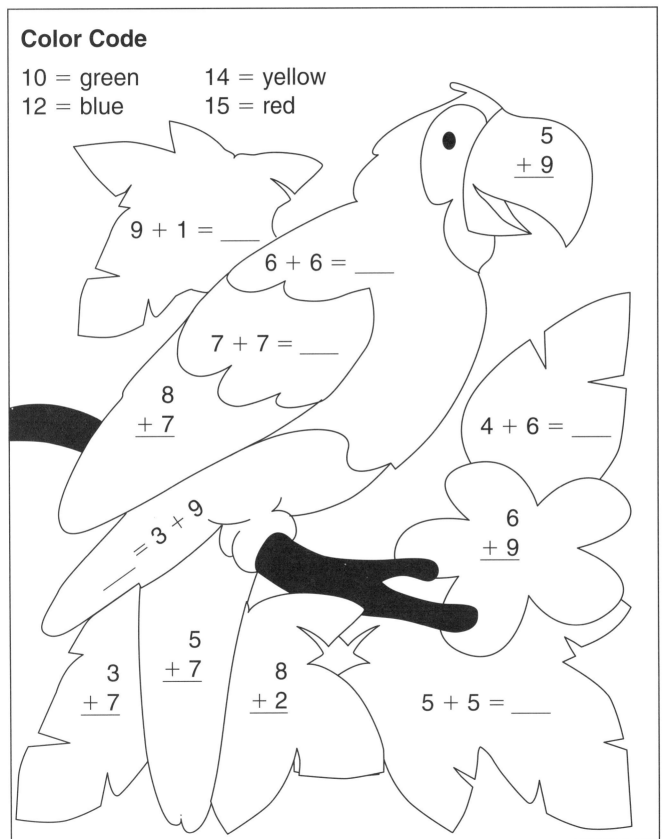

9 + 1 = ___

6 + 6 = ___

7 + 7 = ___

$\begin{array}{r} 8 \\ + 7 \\ \hline \end{array}$

4 + 6 = ___

___ = 3 + 9

$\begin{array}{r} 6 \\ + 9 \\ \hline \end{array}$

$\begin{array}{r} 5 \\ + 9 \\ \hline \end{array}$

$\begin{array}{r} 5 \\ + 7 \\ \hline \end{array}$

$\begin{array}{r} 3 \\ + 7 \\ \hline \end{array}$

$\begin{array}{r} 8 \\ + 2 \\ \hline \end{array}$

5 + 5 = ___

Name-Collection Boxes

Family Note

Today, we began working with name-collection boxes. See the attached letter for more information about this routine.

Please return this Home Link to school tomorrow.

List all the addition facts you know that have a sum of 10.

_____

_____

Write as many names as you can in the name-collection boxes.

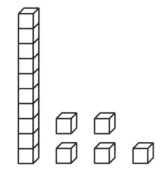

15
10 + 5

18

Family Letter

Name-Collection Boxes

People, things, and ideas often have several different names. For example, Mary calls her parents Mom and Dad. Other people in the family may call them Linda and John, or Aunt Linda and Uncle John, or Grandma and Grandpa. Mail may come addressed to Mr. and Mrs. West. All are names for the same two people.

Your child is bringing home an activity that has a special format for using this naming idea with numbers. We call the format a name-collection box. The box is used for collecting many names for given numbers.

This format offers a simple way for children to understand the idea that numbers can be expressed in many different ways. The open-top box is identified by the name on the label. The box shown here is a 25-box, a name-collection box for the number 25.

Names can include sums, differences, products, quotients, or combinations of operations, as well as words (including words in other languages), tallies, and arrays. A name-collection box can be filled by using any equivalent names.

With repeated practice, children gain the power to rename numbers for a variety of different uses.

25
$37 - 12$ $20 + 5$
~~HHt~~ ~~HHt~~ ~~HHt~~ ~~HHt~~ ~~HHt~~
twenty-five
veinticinco   x x x x x
x x x x x
x x x x x
x x x x x
x x x x x

25-box

Fact Families

Family Note

We have extended our work with facts to subtraction facts by introducing fact families. Your child will generate addition facts and subtraction facts to go with the numbers pictured on the dominoes below.

Note that for the first two problems, there are two addition facts and two subtraction facts. Because the third problem shows a domino with the same number on both halves, there is only one addition fact and one subtraction fact. Ask your child to explain why this is the case.

Please return this Home Link to school tomorrow.

Write the 3 numbers for each domino. Use the numbers to write the fact family.

1. Numbers: _____, _____, _____

Fact family: ___ + ___ = ___   ___ − ___ = ___

___ + ___ = ___   ___ − ___ = ___

2. Numbers: _____, _____, _____

Fact family: ___ + ___ = ___   ___ − ___ = ___

___ + ___ = ___   ___ − ___ = ___

3. Numbers: _____, _____, _____

Fact family: ___ + ___ = ___   ___ − ___ = ___

Fact Triangles

Your child should cut apart the triangles on the other page. Notice that each triangle has the three numbers used in a fact family on it. Use these triangles like flash cards to practice addition and subtraction facts.

The number below the dot is the sum of the other two numbers. For example, 8 is the sum of 5 and 3.

To practice addition, cover the sum. Your child then adds the numbers that are not covered. For example, if you cover 8, your child adds 5 and 3.

To practice subtraction, cover one of the numbers at the bottom of the triangle. Your child then subtracts the uncovered number at the bottom from the sum. For example, if you cover 3, your child subtracts 5 from 8. If you cover 5, your child subtracts 3 from 8.

Fact Triangles have two advantages over regular flash cards.

1. They reinforce the strong link between addition and subtraction.

2. They help simplify the memorizing task by linking four facts together. Knowing a single fact means that you really know four facts.

$$5 + 3 = 8$$
$$3 + 5 = 8$$
$$8 - 5 = 3$$
$$8 - 3 = 5$$

Save this set of Fact Triangles in an envelope or a plastic bag to continue practicing addition and subtraction facts with your child when you have time.

Fact Triangles

Cut out the 6 triangles. Practice the addition and subtraction facts on these triangles with someone at home.

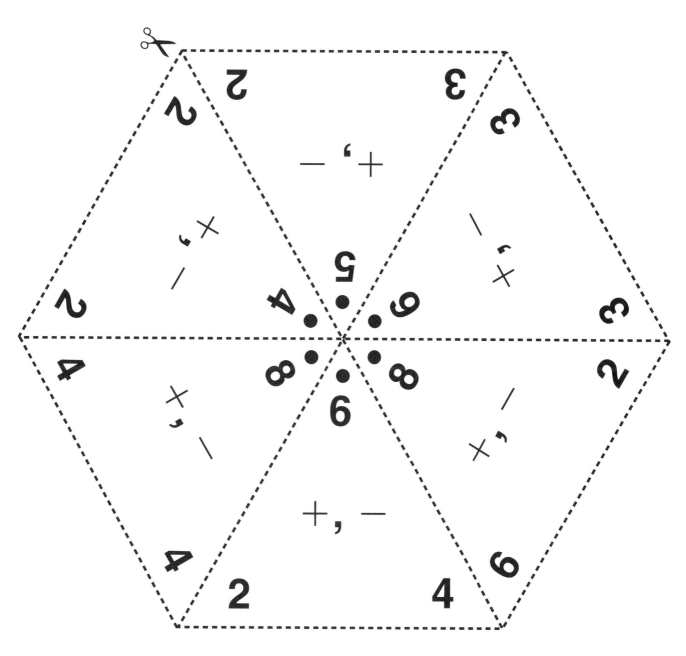

Name _____ Date _____

Fact Routines Practice

Family Note

This Home Link reviews some of the work children have been doing in recent lessons. Note that children are now working with subtraction facts as they are related to addition facts. Encourage your child to include some subtraction "names" in the name-collection box in Problem 3. An example of a subtraction name for the first name-collection-box is $16 - 2$.

Please return this Home Link to school tomorrow.

Write the 3 numbers for the domino. Use the numbers to write the fact family.

1. Numbers: _____, _____, _____

Fact family: ___ + ___ = ___   ___ − ___ = ___

___ + ___ = ___   ___ − ___ = ___

2. Write as many names as you can for 14.

```
┌─ 14 ─────────────┐
│                  │
│                  │
│                  │
│                  │
│                  │
│                  │
│                  │
│                  │
│                  │
└──────────────────┘
```

3. Cross out the names that do not belong.

```
┌─ 20 ─────────────────────┐
│  10 + 10      twenty      │
│                           │
│  H̶H̶T̶ H̶H̶T̶      5 + 5 + 5   │
│                           │
│  2 + 10       15 + 1      │
│                           │
│  20 + 0     ▭▭▭▭▭▭▭▭▭▭    │
│             ▭▭▭▭▭▭▭▭▭▭    │
│  24 − 4                    │
└───────────────────────────┘
```

Use with Lesson 6.5.

Measuring in Centimeters

Family Note

Children are beginning to use metric units to measure length (in addition to the U.S. customary units of inches and feet). Your child should measure the objects to the nearest centimeter. Make sure your child lines up one end of the object being measured with the "0" mark on the ruler.

Please return this Home Link to school tomorrow.

Cut out the ruler. Find four small objects. Draw a picture of each object and measure each object to the nearest centimeter (cm). Record your measurements.

1.

About _____ cm long

2.

About _____ cm long

3.

About _____ cm long

4.

About _____ cm long

0   1   2   3   4   5   6   7   8   9   10   11   12   13   14   15

centimeters

Practicing with Fact Triangles

Family Note

Six more Fact Triangles are being added for practice at home. As you help your child practice with the Fact Triangles, keep the facts your child knows in a separate pile from the facts that still need some work.

Please return this Home Link to school tomorrow.

Cut out the Fact Triangles. Practice these facts at home when you have time. When you are not using the triangles, store them in an envelope or a plastic bag.

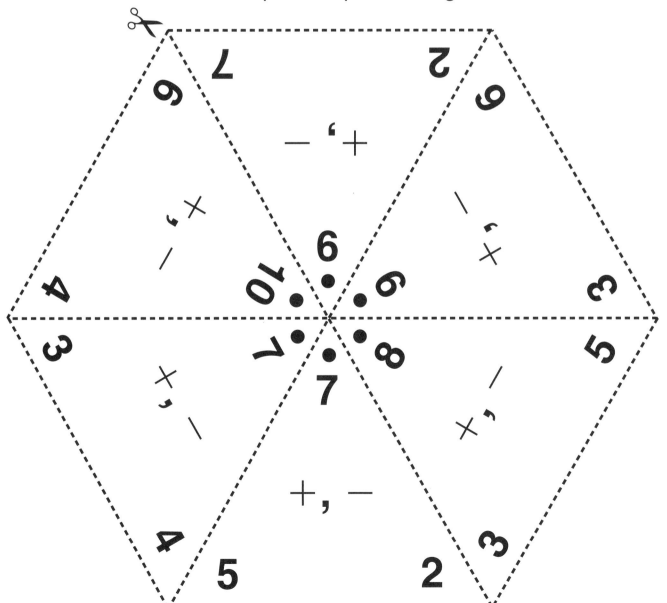

Use with Lesson 6.7.

Counting Coins

Family Note

This Home Link reviews counting combinations of dimes, nickels, and pennies. If your child is having trouble counting coins, you might try the following method:

1. First show the amount with pennies.

2. Then trade the pennies for nickels.

3. Finally, trade the nickels for dimes.

Use real coins if possible.

Children are adding quarters to their work with coins, beginning tomorrow. In preparation for this, please give your child two quarters to bring to school.

Please return this Home Link to school tomorrow.

Use Ⓟ, Ⓝ, and Ⓓ to show each of the amounts in two different ways.

1. 43¢

2. 67¢

3. Ask someone at home for a quarter.

Who is on the Heads side? _____

Complete.

1 quarter = _____ Ⓟ   1 quarter = _____ ¢

1 quarter = _____ Ⓝ

More Counting Coins

Family Note

Children have begun to count coin combinations that include quarters. If your child is having difficulty because the coins are not shown in any particular order, use real coins to model the problems. Sort the coins into groups of like coins (all dimes together, all nickels together) before counting.

   Children are also continuing to use dollars-and-cents notation. If your child has trouble recording amounts in this notation, don't worry—this is a skill we will continue to work on throughout the year.

Please return this Home Link to school tomorrow.

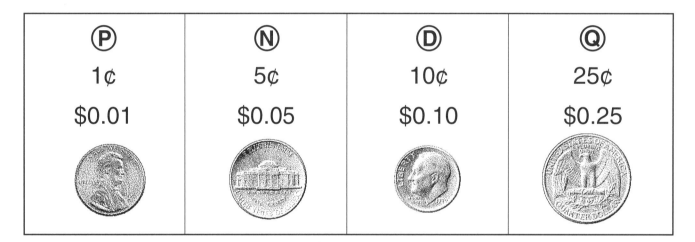

Ⓟ	Ⓝ	Ⓓ	Ⓠ
1¢	5¢	10¢	25¢
$0.01	$0.05	$0.10	$0.25

Count the coins.

Write the total in cents and in dollars-and-cents notation.

1. Ⓠ Ⓓ Ⓝ Ⓝ Ⓝ _____ ¢ or $_____._____

2. Ⓠ Ⓠ Ⓓ Ⓓ Ⓝ Ⓝ Ⓟ Ⓟ _____ ¢ or $_____._____

3. Ⓓ Ⓟ Ⓝ Ⓟ Ⓟ Ⓠ _____ ¢ or $_____._____

4. Ⓟ Ⓝ Ⓝ Ⓠ Ⓟ Ⓠ Ⓓ _____ ¢ or $_____._____

Challenge

5. Ⓟ Ⓠ Ⓠ Ⓝ Ⓓ Ⓓ Ⓝ Ⓝ Ⓠ Ⓓ _____ ¢ or $_____._____

Use with Lesson 6.9.

Time at 5-Minute Intervals

Family Note

In today's lesson children started to work with digital displays of time. Children talked about the number of minutes in an hour and started to tell time at 5-minute intervals. This will require lots of practice, so the *Everyday Mathematics* program will come back to telling time throughout the year.

Please return this Home Link to school tomorrow.

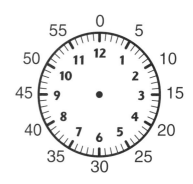

Draw the hour hand and the minute hand.

1.

4:00

2.

7:30

3.

10:15

4. Make up your own.

_____:_____

More Fact Triangles

Family Note

Your child should cut out the triangles on this page. When not using the triangles, store them in the envelope or plastic bag with the first 12 triangles from earlier lessons. As you work with your child, keep a pile of the facts your child knows and a second pile of the facts that still need some work.

Continue practicing addition and subtraction facts at home when you have time.

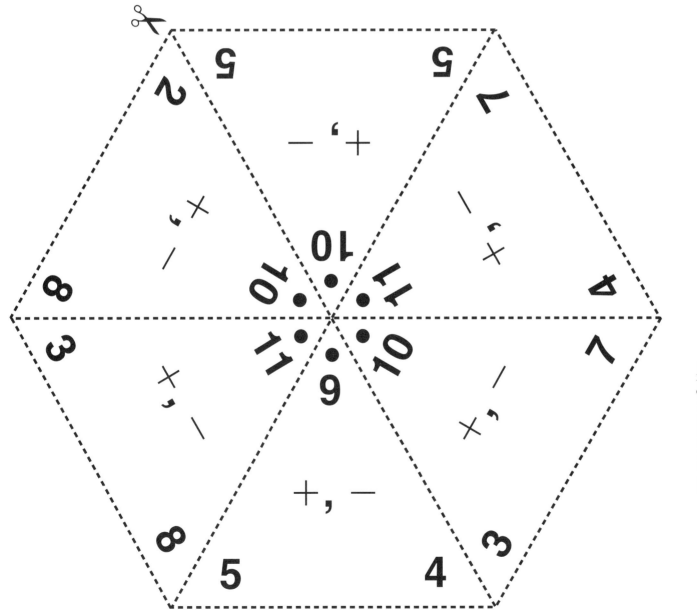

Analyzing a Set of Data

Family Note

Today, we did some calculator counts in class. Ask your child what his or her highest count was at the end of 15 seconds.

Below is a tally chart like one we made in class today. Help your child identify the lowest and the highest counts that someone in Casey's class got. Then help your child find the range of all the counts. (To find the range, subtract the lowest count from the highest count.)

Please return this Home Link to school tomorrow.

Casey's Class Data for Calculator Counts

Counted to	Number of Children
5	/
7	//
10	//// /
11	//// / /
12	////
13	///
15	//
17	/
18	/

1. How many children in Casey's class did the calculator count?

_____

2. Find the highest count.

_____

3. Find the lowest count.

_____

4. Find the range of the counts.

_____

5. If you have a calculator, show someone at home how you did the calculator count. Ask that person to count on the calculator.

Family Letter

Unit 7: Geometry and Attributes

In Unit 7, children will work with 2-dimensional shapes. First, children will classify blocks by their shape, color, and size. Then they will learn to recognize attributes like number of sides and square corners. Later, they will build their own shapes out of straws and twist-ties, identifying the differences among shapes that are polygons and shapes that are not.

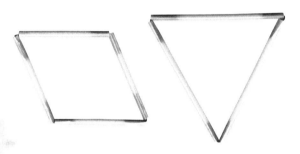

Children will work with 3-dimensional shapes they encounter every day. They will be asked to bring objects from home, which will be organized and labeled to create a "Shapes Museum" for the classroom. For example, a soup can would be labeled "cylinder"; a tennis ball, "sphere." In examining the shapes brought to class, children will begin to identify similarities and differences among five kinds of 3-dimensional shapes: prisms, pyramids, spheres, cylinders, and cones. They will learn to identify characteristics, using terms like *flat* and *round*. We will use the names of the shapes in class, but children will not be expected to memorize their definitions.

In the last lesson of this unit, children will explore symmetry. They will find symmetrical shapes in real life, including butterflies, bells, guitars, vases, and double dominoes. Then they will create their own symmetrical shapes using paper and scissors.

Please keep this Family Letter for reference as your child works through Unit 7.

2-Dimensional Shapes

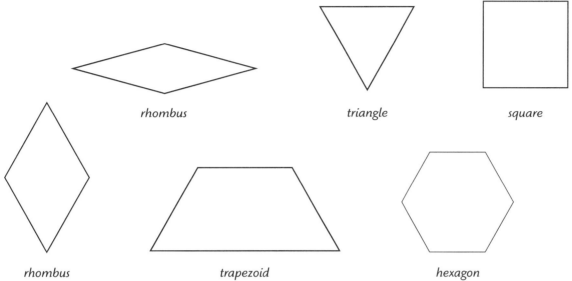

rhombus   *triangle*   *square*

rhombus   *trapezoid*   *hexagon*

3-Dimensional Shapes

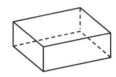

prism A shape with two parallel flat faces (bases) that are the same size and shape. Prisms are classified according to the shape of their two parallel bases. The other sides (also called *faces*) are parallelograms. (A parallelogram is a four-sided polygon with two pairs of parallel sides.) Examples of prisms include books, cereal boxes, and bricks.

pyramid A shape in which one face (the base) is a polygon and the other faces are triangles with a common vertex (corner). (A polygon is a 2-dimensional shape consisting of straight sides that meet only at their ends.) Architectural examples of pyramids include the Transamerica Building in San Francisco, the Temple of the Sun in Peru, and the Pyramids in Egypt.

sphere A shape with a curved surface that is, at all points, the same distance from its center point. A ball is shaped like a sphere.

cylinder A shape with a curved surface and two parallel, circular faces (bases) that are the same size. Examples of cylinders include empty paper towel rolls, coffee cans, and fluorescent lightbulbs.

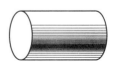

cone A shape with a curved surface, a circular face (base), and one vertex (corner). Examples of cones include cone-shaped party hats, sugar cones served with ice cream, and the orange cones commonly used in road construction.

Use with Lesson 6.13.

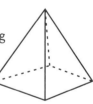

Do-Anytime Activities

To work with your child on the concepts taught in this unit and in previous units, try these interesting and rewarding activities:

1 Draw a name-collection box with a number on the tag. Ask your child to write at least 10 equivalent names for the given number.

2 Occasionally ask questions about time: What time is it? What time will it be in five minutes? In ten minutes? In one hour?

3 Continue to work on addition and subtraction facts using Fact Triangles, short drill sessions, and any of the games introduced at school.

4 If a calculator is available, ask your child to show you how to count with it. See how high your child can count on the calculator.

5 Look for geometric shapes around the house, at the supermarket, as part of architectural features, and on street signs. Begin to call these shapes by their geometric names.

12
17 − 5
2 + 10
4 + 8
13 − 1
twelve
doce
⧸⧸⧸⧸ ⧸⧸⧸⧸ //

Use with Lesson 6.13.

Building Skills through Games

In Unit 7, your child will practice place-value and classification skills by playing the following games:

Attribute Train Game

One player puts down a block. The next player finds a block that differs in only one attribute—shape, size, or color—from the first block and puts it next to the first block. Each player continues to add to the "train" of blocks.

Tens-and-Ones Trading Game

Players take turns putting base-10 blocks on their Tens-and-Ones Mat according to the roll of a die. Whenever possible, they exchange 10 cubes for 1 long. The first player to get 10 longs wins!

Hundreds	Tens	Ones	Place-Value Mat

As You Help Your Child with Homework

As your child brings home assignments, you may want to go over the instructions together, clarifying them as necessary. The answers listed below will guide you through this unit's Home Links.

Home Link 7.3

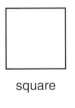
square

rhombus

hexagon

trapezoid

triangle

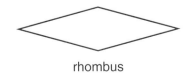
rhombus

Home Link 7.4

1.

2. Sample drawing:

3. Sample drawing:

Use with Lesson 6.13.

Practicing with Fact Triangles

Cut out these Fact Triangles.

Practice the facts at home.

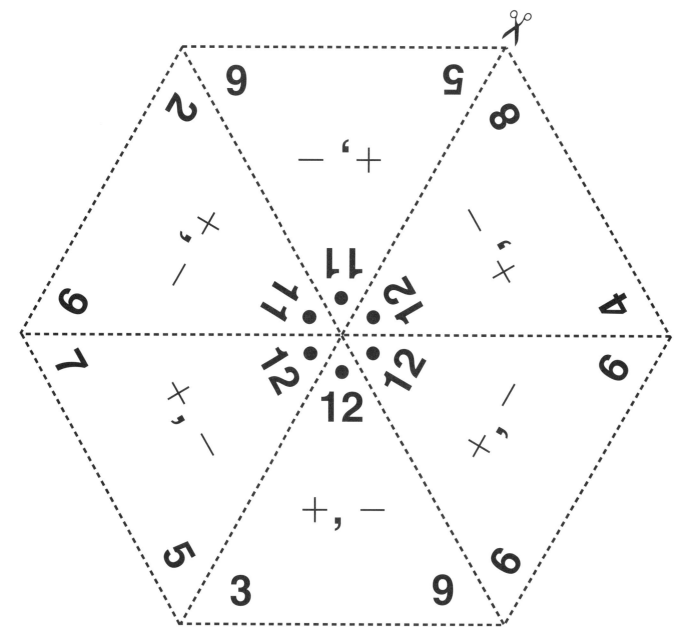

Use with Lesson 7.1.

Shapes

Family Note

The class has been identifying and comparing three attributes of objects: shape, color, and size. We are going to work with 2-dimensional and 3-dimensional shapes in future lessons. In preparation for this, help your child find objects with the shapes listed. Also help your child find things to bring to school for our Shapes Museum. They should not be valuable or breakable.

Please return this Home Link to school tomorrow.

1. Find something in your house that has a triangle in it. Write its name or draw its picture.

2. Find something in your house that has a circle in it. Write its name or draw its picture.

3. Find something in your house that has a square in it. Write its name or draw its picture.

4. Starting tomorrow, bring things to school for the Shapes Museum. You might bring in boxes, soup cans, balls, party hats, pyramids, and any other shapes you can find. Get permission to bring things that are not yours.

Polygons

Family Note

We are beginning to identify polygons and their characteristics. In today's lesson, we made designs with blocks shaped like the polygons on this page.

On this page, your child will try to name the shapes we worked with today. Expect that some of the names may still be confusing. Help your child find designs at home that repeat the shapes on this page; for example, floor tiles repeat a square over and over again.

Please return this Home Link to school tomorrow.

Use the word bank to help you write the name for each shape.

Word Bank				
hexagon	rhombus	square	trapezoid	triangle

_____   _____   _____

_____   _____   _____

Find patterns or repeating designs at home that have pattern-block shapes in them. Draw one of these patterns or designs on the back of this page.

Write where you found this pattern. Have someone help you.

Use with Lesson 7.3.

Name   Date

Family Note

This Home Link follows up our work in class identifying shapes called polygons. The sides of a polygon are all straight. Polygons have corners where two sides meet. Sides meet only at their ends. The sides are connected—there aren't any gaps. Help your child identify the polygons below.

Please return this Home Link to school tomorrow.

1. Circle all the shapes below that are polygons.

Challenge

2. Draw a shape that is NOT on this page, and IS a polygon.

3. Draw a shape that is NOT on this page, and IS NOT a polygon.

Practicing with Fact Triangles

Family Note

Your child should cut apart the triangles on this page. Add these to the envelope or plastic bag with the Fact Triangles from earlier lessons. As you show the triangles, make a pile of the facts your child knows and a second pile of the facts that still need work.

Continue practicing addition and subtraction facts at home.

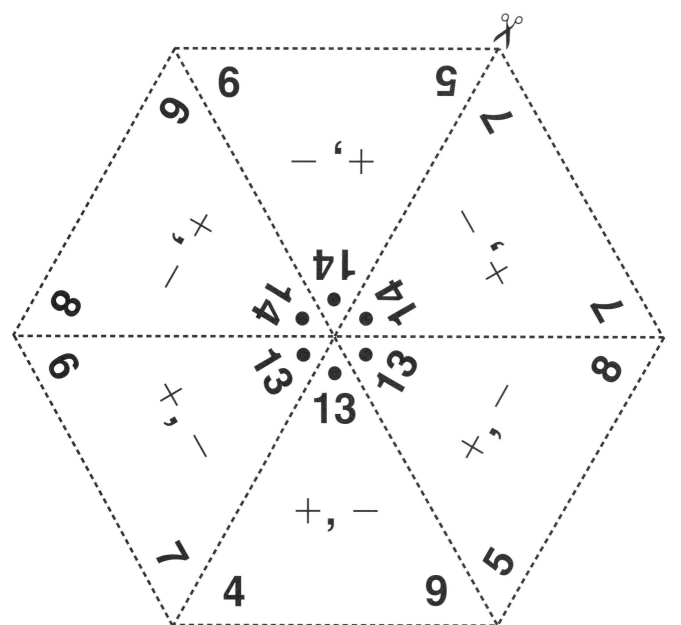

Tracing Shapes

Family Note

The class has been working with 2-dimensional and 3-dimensional shapes. For today's Home Link, help your child find 3-dimensional objects, and then help him or her trace around one surface of each object—for example, the bottom of a box, the bottom of a can, the bottom of a cup, and so on. Use the front and back of this sheet, and other sheets if you want. For each tracing, help your child find a name for the shape in the Word Bank, and write the name on the tracing.

Please return this Home Link to school tomorrow.

Find 3-dimensional shapes with flat faces (sides).

On the front and back of this page trace around one face of each shape.

Write the name of the shape.

Word Bank

square

trapezoid

not a polygon

circle

rhombus

rectangle

hexagon

triangle

other polygon

Finding Symmetry in Nature

Family Note

A picture or object has symmetry if it can be folded in half so that the two halves match exactly. In today's lesson, the class explored symmetry by cutting out designs from folded paper. To continue our exploration of symmetry, help your child find pictures that show symmetry in nature. For example: pictures of butterflies, leaves, animal markings, flowers, snowflakes, and so on.

Please return this Home Link to school tomorrow.

Find symmetrical pictures in magazines.

Cut out your favorite pictures and glue them onto this page.

Use with Lesson 7.7.

Unit 8: Mental Arithmetic, Money, and Fractions

In Unit 8, children will examine a dollar bill and add the dollar to the money units they already know. They will continue to count and record amounts of money (using pennies, nickels, dimes, and quarters), often in more than one way. They will also begin learning how to make change.

Children will also create addition, subtraction, and comparison problems for the class to solve and will share their own problem-solving strategies. Having children share their solution strategies is emphasized in *Everyday Mathematics* and helps children feel more confident as they express their ideas.

Later in this unit, children will work with fractions. They will be reminded that fractions are equal parts of wholes. When dealing with fractions, it is important that children keep in mind the "whole" or the ONE to which the fraction is linked. For example, $\frac{1}{2}$ of an apple and $\frac{1}{2}$ of a dollar are not the same, because they deal with different types of "wholes."

$\frac{7}{12}$ of my creature is blue.

Please keep this Family Letter for reference as your child works through Unit 8.

Vocabulary

Important terms in Unit 8:

fractional parts Equal parts of any whole.
For example:

Half $\left(\frac{1}{2}\right)$ of the objects that make
up a whole set are broken.

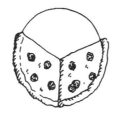

One of three parts $\left(\frac{1}{3}\right)$
of a whole has been eaten.

near doubles A strategy derived from the "doubles"
facts. For example, a child might solve 3 + 4 by noting
that 3 + 3 = 6, so 3 + 4 must be 1 more than 6.

Building Skills through Games

In Unit 8, your child will practice addition, place value, and money skills by playing
the following games:

Addition Top-It

Players turn over two cards and call out the sum.
The player with the higher sum keeps all the cards.
The player with more cards at the end wins!

Base-10 Exchange

Players roll the dice and put that number of cubes on
their Place-Value Mats. Whenever possible, they
exchange 10 cubes for 1 long. The first player to make
an exchange for a flat wins!

flat   long cube

1 flat = 10 longs = 100 cubes

One-Dollar Exchange

Players roll the dice and put that number of cents on their Place-Value Mats.
Whenever possible, they exchange 10 pennies for 1 dime. The first player to make
an exchange for a $1 bill wins!

Use with Lesson 7.8.

Do-Anytime Activities

To work with your child on the concepts taught in this unit and in previous units, try these interesting and rewarding activities:

1 Continue to review addition and subtraction facts.

2 Ask questions like the following:

▶ I want to buy an airplane that costs 27 cents. If I give the clerk 3 dimes, how much change will I get back?

▶ How can you show 14 cents using exactly 6 coins? (Have the actual coins available.)

▶ How many different ways can you show 14 cents? (Have the actual coins available.)

3 Count out 8 pennies (or any type of counter, such as beans or macaroni). Ask your child to show you $\frac{1}{2}$ of the pennies and then $\frac{1}{4}$ of the pennies. Do this with a variety of different numbers.

4 Encourage your child to count various collections of coins you may have accumulated.

As You Help Your Child with Homework

As your child brings home assignments, you may want to go over the instructions together, clarifying them as necessary. The answers listed below will guide you through this unit's Home Links.

Home Link 8.1

3. September: 52¢, or $0.52

October: 61¢, or $0.61

November: 96¢, or $0.96

December: 88¢, or $0.88

4. 297¢, or $2.97

Home Link 8.2

3. 81¢, or $0.81   **4.** 125¢, or $1.25

Home Link 8.3

1. 569   **2.** 843   **3.** 709

4. 465   **5.** Answers vary.

Home Link 8.5

1. 3 dimes; 4 cents in change

2. 8 dimes; 7 cents in change

3. 10 dimes; 5 cents in change

Home Link 8.7

1.

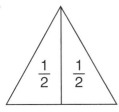 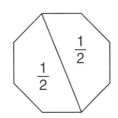

2. 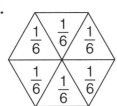   **3.**

Home Link 8.8

1. 5   **2.** 4   **3.** 4

Home Link 8.9

1. $4 + 6 = 10$

2. $9 + 1 = 10$

3. $9 + 9 = 18$

4. $3 + 7 = 10$

$7 + 3 = 10$

$10 - 3 = 7$

$10 - 7 = 3$

5. $4 + 4 = 8$

$8 - 4 = 4$

6. $1 + 6 = 7$

$6 + 1 = 7$

$7 - 1 = 6$

$7 - 6 = 1$

Use with Lesson 7.8.

Coin Combinations

Family Note

In the next lesson, we will extend our work with money to include dollars. In preparation for this, we have been practicing counting coins. If your child has difficulty with some problems on this page, use real coins to model the situations. Arrange the coins into groups of like coins and count the coins of the highest value first.

Please return this Home Link to school tomorrow.

1. Mark the coins you need to buy an eraser.

2. Mark the coins you need to buy a box of crayons.

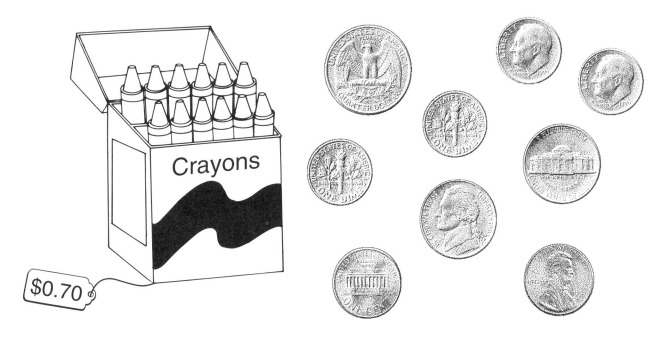

Coin Combinations (cont.)

3. Melanie saved her money. How much did she save each month?

September

Total: _____

October

Total: _____

November

Total: _____

December

Total: _____

Challenge

4. How much did Melanie save in all? _____

Dollars and More

Family Note

Today we took a close look at a dollar bill. Since we have only begun to work with dollars, some of the problems on this page may be difficult for your child. If possible, use real money to model the problems. Start by counting the bills and coins in the example with your child.

Please return this Home Link to school tomorrow.

Show how you would pay for each item. Use $1, ⓟ, ⓝ, ⓓ, or ⓠ.

Example

$1.95

$1 ⓠ ⓠ ⓠ ⓓ ⓓ

1.

$2.85

2.

$3.24

3. Write this amount in two ways.

ⓠ ⓠ ⓝ ⓓ ⓝ ⓓ ⓟ

Total: _____ $_____._____.

On the back of the page, show this amount with different coins.

Challenge

4. ⓝ ⓓ ⓓ ⓓ ⓝ ⓓ ⓠ ⓠ ⓠ

Total: _____ $_____._____.

More Riddles

Family Note

We are extending our work with base-10 blocks to include 100s. The base-10 block for 100 is called a "flat." Note that the blocks are not always shown in the same order. If your child finds some of the problems difficult, you might model them with dollar bills (for flats), dimes (for longs), and pennies (for cubes). These make good substitutes for base-10 blocks. Ask your child to explain why there is a zero in the number in Problem 3. To practice reading 3-digit numbers, ask your child to read his or her answers to you.

Please return this Home Link to school tomorrow.

Hundreds	Tens	Ones

Solve the riddles. ***Example***

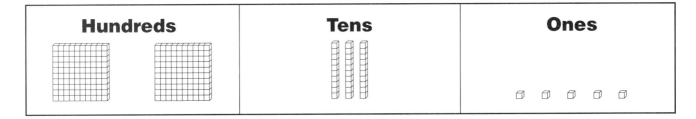

2 ▨s   5 ▯s   7 ▱s   What am I? __257__

1.
5 ▨s   6 ▯s   9 ▱s   What am I? _____

2.
4 ▯s   8 ▨s   3 ▱s   What am I? _____

3. 7 hundreds and 9 ones.   What am I? _____

Challenge

4. 3 hundreds, 16 tens, 5 ones.   What am I? _____

5. Make up your own riddle. Ask someone at home to solve it.

Use with Lesson 8.3.

A Shopping Story

Family Note

We have been practicing addition of 2-digit numbers with number stories about money. Please help your child find pictures of two items in a magazine, newspaper, or catalog that each cost less than one dollar. (Newspaper inserts tend to be a good source for such items.) Ask your child to make up and tell you a number story to go with the items.

Please return this Home Link to school tomorrow.

Sample Story

I bought a ball and an eraser. I paid 52 cents.

Number model $35¢ + 17¢ = 52¢$

Glue or tape your pictures below or on the back of this page. Write your story.

Number model _____

Making Change

Family Note

Children are beginning to learn to make change. If you have dimes, nickels, and pennies available, have your child act out the problems with real money. For each problem, your child should pay with just enough dimes to cover the cost.

Please return this Home Link to school tomorrow.

Record the number of dimes you paid. Record the amount of change you got.

Example	**1.**	**2.**
47¢	26¢	5¢
marbles	balloon	toy car

I paid with	I paid with	I paid with
__5__ dimes.	____ dimes.	____ dimes.
I got __3__ cents in change.	I got ____ cents in change.	I got ____ cents in change.

Challenge

3. I paid with ____ dimes.

    I got ____ cents in change.

Use with Lesson 8.5.

Exploring Halves and Fourths

Family Note

We are beginning to explore the concept of fractions. Today, children focused on identifying fractional parts of things. We emphasized that fractional parts come from dividing something into equal parts.

Help your child collect the items listed below.

Please return this Home Link to school tomorrow.

1. Fill a glass so that it is about half full. Then fill another glass of the same size so that it is about half empty. Is there a difference? _____

2. Divide each of the squares in half. Try to divide each square in a different way.

3. Divide each of the squares into fourths. Try to divide each square in a different way.

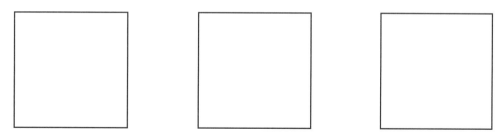

4. Bring one-half of something to school tomorrow. Some examples: one-half of an apple, one-half of a sandwich, one-half of a leaf, one-half of a newspaper page.

5. Also, bring one-fourth of something.

Equal Parts

Family Note

Ask your child to explain how he or she knows which figures are divided into equal fractional parts. Then help your child write fractions in the equal parts.

Please return this Home Link to school tomorrow.

Fill in the ovals below the shapes that show equal parts.
Write fractions in the equal parts.

1.

halves

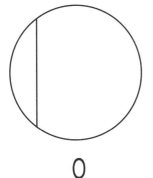   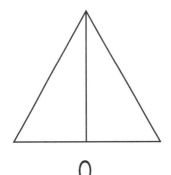

O   O   O

2.

sixths

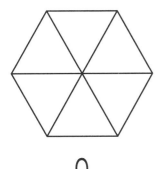   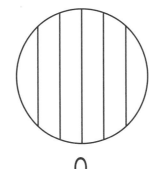   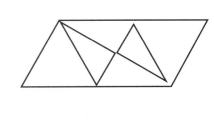

O   O   O

3.

fourths

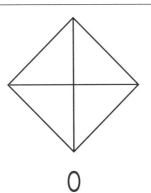   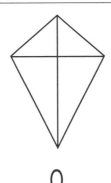   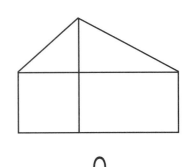

O   O   O

Use with Lesson 8.7.

Name _____   Date _____

Sharing Sets of Objects

Family Note

Today we extended our work with fractions to finding fractional parts of a collection of objects. Help your child act out the problems below with pennies or counters. When sharing things equally, one strategy is to distribute the things just as you would deal cards in a card game, and then count the things in one share. In Problem 4, your child should recognize that if 15 pennies are shared equally by 6 children, there will be 3 leftover pennies.

Please return this Home Link to school tomorrow.

Use pennies to help you solve the problems.

1. Halves: 2 people share 10 pennies equally.
Circle each person's share.

Ⓟ Ⓟ Ⓟ Ⓟ Ⓟ Ⓟ Ⓟ Ⓟ Ⓟ Ⓟ

How many pennies does each person get? _____

2. Thirds: 3 children share 12 balloons equally.
Draw the balloons each child gets.

How many balloons does each child get? _____

3. Fourths: 4 children share 16 flowers equally.
How many flowers does each child get? _____

Challenge

4. Explain to someone at home what happens if 6 children share 15 pennies equally.

Use with Lesson 8.8.

Facts Practice

Family Note

Continue to practice simple addition facts at home. The goal is for your child to memorize the + 0, + 1, doubles facts, and sums that equal 10 by the end of this school year.

Please return this Home Link to school tomorrow.

Fill in the missing numbers.

1.

_____ + 6 = _____

2.

_____ + 1 = _____

3.

_____ + _____ = _____

Write the fact family below each triangle.

4.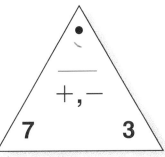

_____ + _____ = _____

_____ + _____ = _____

_____ − _____ = _____

_____ − _____ = _____

5.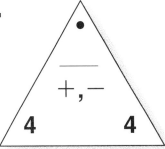

_____ + _____ = _____

_____ + _____ = _____

_____ − _____ = _____

_____ − _____ = _____

6.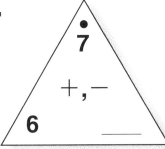

_____ + _____ = _____

_____ + _____ = _____

_____ − _____ = _____

_____ − _____ = _____

Use with Lesson 8.9.

Unit 9: Place Value and Fractions

The concept of place value (ones, tens, hundreds, and so on) that children have worked on since *Kindergarten Everyday Mathematics* will be taught on a more formal level in this unit. Patterns on number grids will be used to reinforce place-value concepts. For example, children may be asked to identify a hidden number on the number grid and to describe the strategies used to find and name that number. Once they are able to do this, they will solve number-grid puzzles, which are pieces of a number grid with all but a few numbers missing. Here are a few examples of number-grid puzzles:

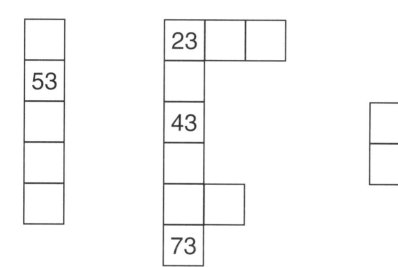

Children know that all numbers are written with one or more of only 10 digits: 0, 1, 2, 3, 4, 5, 6, 7, 8, and 9. In order to reinforce this understanding, children will identify the place value of the different digits in 2- and 3-digit numbers. Help your child remember that these same digits are also used to express quantities less than 1 with decimals or fractions.

Later in this unit, children will extend their understanding of fraction concepts as they see relationships among fraction words, meanings, and symbols.

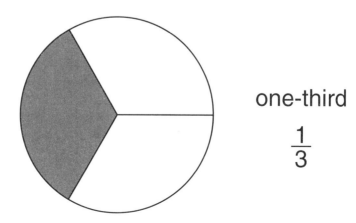

one-third

$\frac{1}{3}$

Vocabulary

Important terms in Unit 9:

numerator and **denominator** Parts of a fraction.

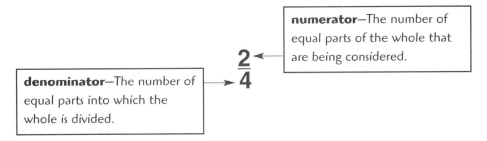

numerator—The number of equal parts of the whole that are being considered.

denominator—The number of equal parts into which the whole is divided.

$$\frac{2}{4}$$

2-digit numbers Numbers from 10 through 99 have two digits each.

3-digit numbers Numbers from 100 through 999 have three digits each.

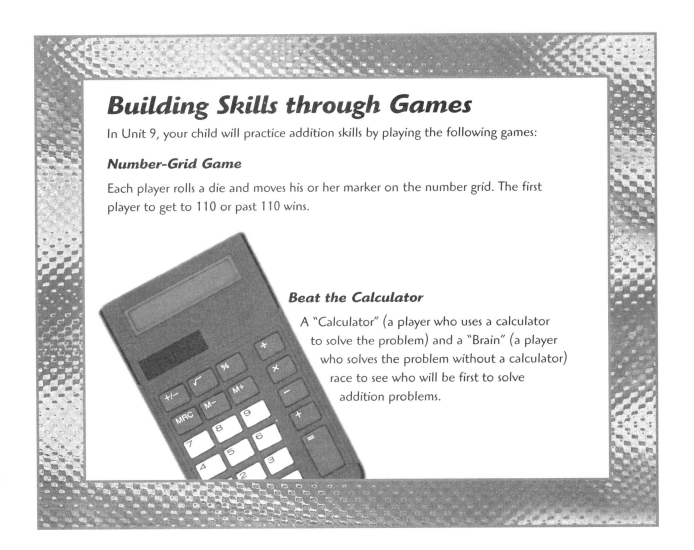

Building Skills through Games

In Unit 9, your child will practice addition skills by playing the following games:

Number-Grid Game

Each player rolls a die and moves his or her marker on the number grid. The first player to get to 110 or past 110 wins.

Beat the Calculator

A "Calculator" (a player who uses a calculator to solve the problem) and a "Brain" (a player who solves the problem without a calculator) race to see who will be first to solve addition problems.

Use with Lesson 8.10.

Do-Anytime Activities

To work with your child on concepts taught in this unit and in previous units, try these interesting and rewarding activities:

1 Ask questions, such as the following: *What is the fraction word for each of 4 equal parts of something?* (fourths) *Each of eight equal parts?* (eighths)

2 Give your child several pieces of paper to fold into halves, fourths, or eighths. He or she can label each part with the appropriate fraction symbol $(\frac{1}{2}, \frac{1}{4}, \frac{1}{8})$.

3 Using a set of numbers, have your child write the largest and smallest 2- and 3-digit whole numbers possible. For example, using 5, 2, and 9, the largest whole number is 952; the smallest is 259.

4 Say a 2- or 3-digit number. Then have your child identify the actual value of the digit in each place. For example, in the number 952, the value of the 9 is 900, the value of the 5 is 50, and the value of the 2 is 2 ones, or two. An important goal of *Everyday Mathematics* is for children eventually to think of any digit in a multidigit number by its place-value name.

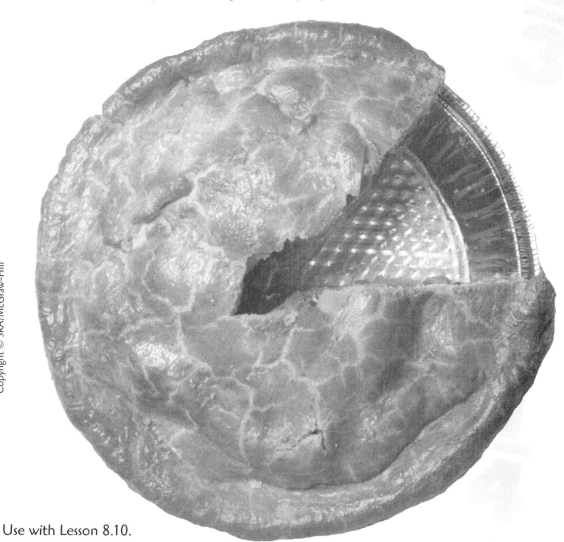

Use with Lesson 8.10.

As You Help Your Child with Homework

As your child brings home assignments, you may want to go over the instructions together, clarifying them as necessary. The answers listed below will guide you through this unit's Home Links.

Home Link 9.2

1. 41	**2.** 71	**3.** 23
4. 72	**5.** 78	**6.** 66
7. 65	**8.** 79	**9.** 38
10. 34	**11.** 21	**12.** 93

Home Link 9.3

1.
```
43
53
63
73
83
```

2.
```
23 24 25
33
   43
   53
   63 64
   73
```

3.
```
      59
      69
78 79 80
88 89 90
```

4.
```
22
32
   43
   53
      64
      74
```

5.
```
53    55
   64
73    75
```

Home Link 9.4

1. |||||||...........77
2. |||||...........58

3. 71 **4.** 75 **5.** 59

Home Link 9.6

1. $\frac{1}{5}$ **2.** $\frac{2}{3}$ **3.** $\frac{5}{6}$

4.   **5.**

6.

Home Link 9.7

2. $\frac{1}{3}$ **3.** $\frac{1}{4}$ **4.** $\frac{5}{8}$

Home Link 9.8

1.   **2.**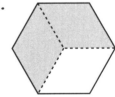

3.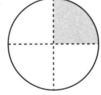

4. hexagon, square
5. 2
6. 3 pennies

Use with Lesson 8.10.

Number-Grid Hunt

Home Link 9.1

Family Note

Ask your child to describe some of the patterns in the number grid below. Then ask him or her to fill in specific numbers you suggest. For example: where would the number 140 go? Do this with a few other numbers before your child completes the rest of the grid. By learning to identify and use patterns in the number grid, your child will develop a strong number sense as well as computation skills.

Please return this Home Link to school tomorrow.

Ask someone to say a number. Record it on the number grid. Do this for several numbers. Then finish filling in the grid on your own.

101									
			125						
							139		
									150
171									
	183								

Using the Number Grid

Family Note

Ask your child to explain how to count up and back by 10s on the number grid and then to demonstrate how to solve the addition and subtraction problems on the number grid. If your child counts one space at a time, remind him or her that to count up by 10s, you can move down one row for every 10 and to count back by 10s, you can move up one row for every 10.

Please return this Home Link to school tomorrow.

Use the number grid to solve the problems.

									0
1	2	3	4	5	6	7	8	9	10
11	12	13	14	15	16	17	18	19	20
21	22	23	24	25	26	27	28	29	30
31	32	33	34	35	36	37	38	39	40
41	42	43	44	45	46	47	48	49	50
51	52	53	54	55	56	57	58	59	60
61	62	63	64	65	66	67	68	69	70
71	72	73	74	75	76	77	78	79	80
81	82	83	84	85	86	87	88	89	90
91	92	93	94	95	96	97	98	99	100

1. $35 + 6 =$ ____

2. $61 + 10 =$ ____

3. $43 - 20 =$ ____

4. ____ $= 82 - 10$ **5.** ____ $= 58 + 20$ **6.** ____ $= 75 - 9$

7. $\begin{array}{r} 55 \\ + 10 \\ \hline \end{array}$ **8.** $\begin{array}{r} 99 \\ - 20 \\ \hline \end{array}$ **9.** $\begin{array}{r} 46 \\ - 8 \\ \hline \end{array}$

Challenge

10. $\begin{array}{r} 84 \\ - 50 \\ \hline \end{array}$ **11.** $\begin{array}{r} 39 \\ - 18 \\ \hline \end{array}$ **12.** ____ $= 62 + 31$

Number-Grid Puzzles

Family Note

Have your child show you how to complete the number-grid pieces. Encourage him or her to explain patterns in the number grid that are helpful for solving the problems. For example if you move up one row, the digit in the 10s place is 1 less.

Please return this Home Link to school tomorrow.

Show someone at home how to fill in the missing numbers.

1.

53

2.

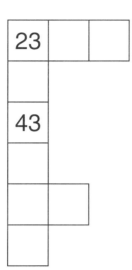

23

43

3.

79

Challenge

4. 22

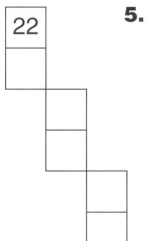

5.

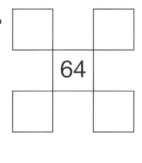

64

									0
1	2	3	4	5	6	7	8	9	10
11	12	13	14	15	16	17	18	19	20
21	22	23	24	25	26	27	28	29	30
31	32	33	34	35	36	37	38	39	40
41	42	43	44	45	46	47	48	49	50
51	52	53	54	55	56	57	58	59	60
61	62	63	64	65	66	67	68	69	70
71	72	73	74	75	76	77	78	79	80
81	82	83	84	85	86	87	88	89	90
91	92	93	94	95	96	97	98	99	100

Name   Date

Solving Problems Two Ways

**Family
Note**

Ask your child to explain how to solve the first set of problems with   52
base-10 blocks and the second set on the number grid. Please do   + 35
not teach your child a formal algorithm for addition, as shown in   ——
margin. It is important that children at this stage work with more   87
concrete representations. This will be beneficial later on, when they
are faced with more difficult problems.

Please return this Home Link to school tomorrow.

Show the total number of base-10 blocks. Then write the total.

Example |||||.. + |||..... = ||||||||.......

   52   +   35   =   87

1. |..... + ||||||.. =

   15   +   62   =   _____

2. |||.... + ||.... =

   34   +   24   =   _____

Use the number grid to help you solve the problems.

3. 63 + 8 = ____

4. 55 + 20 = ____

5. ____ = 47 + 12

									0
1	2	3	4	5	6	7	8	9	10
11	12	13	14	15	16	17	18	19	20
21	22	23	24	25	26	27	28	29	30
31	32	33	34	35	36	37	38	39	40
41	42	43	44	45	46	47	48	49	50
51	52	53	54	55	56	57	58	59	60
61	62	63	64	65	66	67	68	69	70
71	72	73	74	75	76	77	78	79	80
81	82	83	84	85	86	87	88	89	90
91	92	93	94	95	96	97	98	99	100

Use with Lesson 9.4.

Symmetry

Family Note

In class today, children used blocks to make the mirror image of a design across a line of symmetry. This resulted in a symmetrical design. A figure is symmetrical across a line if it has two matching halves. On this page, help your child complete the designs so that they are symmetrical.

Please return this Home Link to school tomorrow.

Complete each design so the two halves will match.

Example

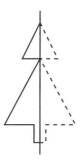

1.

2.

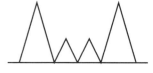

3.

4.

5.

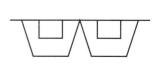

6. Which completed design shows a letter of the alphabet?

7. Draw a design of your own on one side of a line. Complete the design on the other side of the line. When you fold on the line the two halves should match. Use the back of this page.

Fractional Parts

Family Note

In Unit 8, we worked with unit fractions, such as $\frac{1}{2}$, $\frac{1}{3}$, and $\frac{1}{4}$. Today, we started to explore fractions in which the number above the fraction bar is more than 1, such as $\frac{2}{3}$, $\frac{3}{4}$, and $\frac{5}{6}$. If your child is having trouble with some of the problems on this page, you might mention that $\frac{1}{2}$ means that 1 out of 2 parts is shaded, that $\frac{3}{6}$ means that 3 out of 6 parts are shaded, and so on. Or you might ask your child to explain the fractions to you in this way.

Please return this Home Link to school tomorrow.

Mark the fraction that tells what part of the circle is shaded.

1.
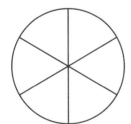

$\frac{1}{2}$ $\frac{5}{6}$

$\frac{1}{5}$ $\frac{5}{1}$

2.
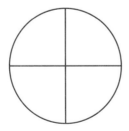

$\frac{2}{2}$ $\frac{2}{3}$

$\frac{3}{4}$ $\frac{3}{1}$

3.
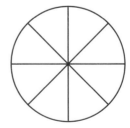

$\frac{1}{6}$ $\frac{1}{5}$

$\frac{6}{5}$ $\frac{5}{6}$

Shade the circles.

4.
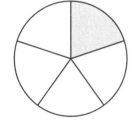

Shade $\frac{4}{6}$.

5.

Shade $\frac{3}{4}$.

6.
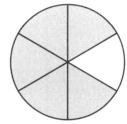

Shade $\frac{5}{8}$.

Challenge

7. Find 2 circles on this page that have the same fraction of the whole shaded. Mark them with an X.

Comparing Fractions

Family Note

Today we divided unit strips into equal parts: halves, thirds, fourths, sixths, and eighths. Then we compared the sizes of the parts. Your child probably cannot tell which of two fractions is more by looking at the fractions, but he or she should be able to compare two fractions by looking at pictures of them. Encourage your child to label one part of each shape with a fraction before deciding which fraction is more or less.

Please return this Home Link to school tomorrow.

1. Which would you rather have, half of candy bar A or half of candy bar B? Explain your answer to someone at home.

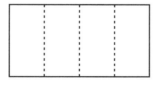

2. Which is more, $\frac{1}{5}$ or $\frac{1}{3}$?

_____

3. Which is more, $\frac{1}{4}$ or $\frac{1}{6}$?

_____

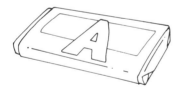

Challenge

4. Which is less, $\frac{3}{4}$ or $\frac{5}{8}$?

_____

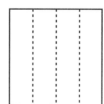   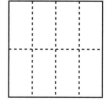

Solving Fraction Problems

Family Note

This Home Link reviews some of the fraction concepts we have covered this year. The most important concept first graders should understand is that a fraction names a part of something (the whole) that has been divided into equal parts. Because for many children the work this year is a first exposure to fraction concepts, they may still be unclear about some of the ideas we have explored. That's okay; these and other fraction concepts will be revisited in later grades.

Please return this Home Link to school tomorrow.

1. Shade $\frac{1}{4}$ of the circle.

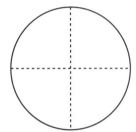

2. Shade $\frac{2}{3}$ of the hexagon.

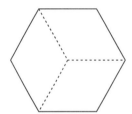

3. Shade $\frac{5}{8}$ of the square.

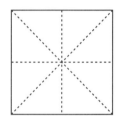

4. Circle the names of the shapes for which you shaded more than $\frac{1}{2}$ of the shape.

    circle   hexagon   square

5. Divide the rectangle into fourths.
Shade $\frac{1}{2}$ of the rectangle.
How many fourths did you shade? _____

6. Four friends share 12 pennies equally.
Circle the number of pennies that each friend gets.

Family Letter

Unit 10: **End-of-Year Reviews and Assessments**

In Unit 10, children will review the concepts and skills they have learned throughout the year. Children will review ways to make sense of collections of data, such as height measurements. Specifically, they will use the data they collected at the beginning of the year to calculate how much they have grown during the last few months.

Children will also continue to use mental math strategies to solve number stories involving money.

Finally, children will review the following skills:

· Telling time to 5 minutes on an analog clock

· Using straws to construct geometric figures

· Reading and comparing temperatures on a thermometer

· Understanding place-value concepts

· Using the number grid

Do-Anytime Activities

To work with your child on the concepts reviewed in this unit, try these interesting and rewarding activities:

1 Continue to work on telling time to the minute.

2 Ask for answers to number stories that involve two or more items. *For example:* I want to buy a donut for 45 cents and a juice box for 89 cents. How much money do I need? ($1.34) Encourage your child to use mental math, coins, the number line, or the number grid to work out solutions.

3 Point to a 3-digit number, such as 528. Ask what the digit "2" means (20); the "5" (500); the "8" (8).

4 Have your child create the largest and smallest numbers given 3 digits.

5 Together, note the thermometer temperature when the weather feels too hot, too cold, or about right. Encourage your child to read any temperature sign or billboard when you travel, noting whether the degrees are Celsius or Fahrenheit.

Use with Lesson 9.9.

Building Skills through Games

In this unit, your child will practice addition and money skills by playing the following games:

Beat the Calculator

A "Calculator" (a player who uses a calculator to solve the problem) and a "Brain" (a player who solves the problem without a calculator) race to see who will be first to solve addition problems.

Buyer and Vendor Game

Players take turns being the "Buyer" and the "Vending Machine." The "Buyer" gives the "Vending Machine" the correct amount in coins for the purchase of an item. The "Vending Machine" determines if the coin combination is correct.

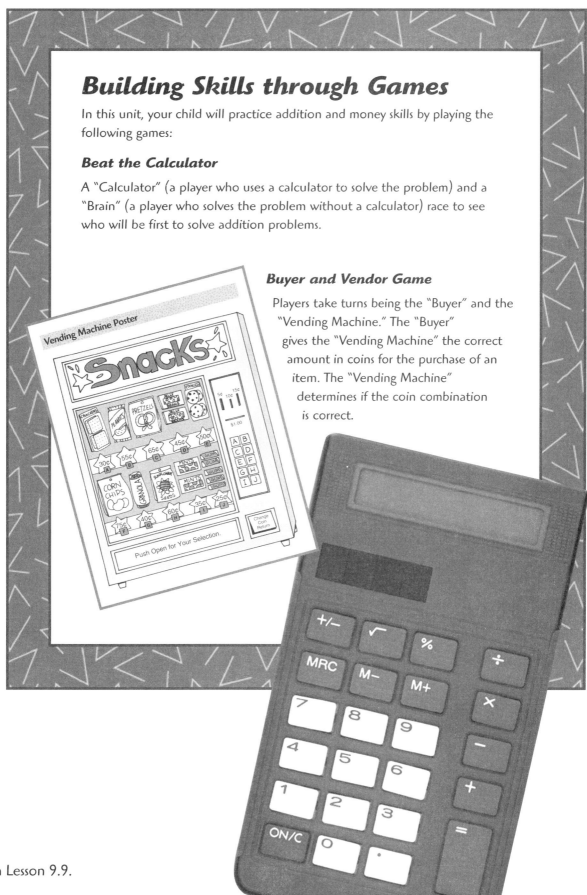

Use with Lesson 9.9.

Unit 3 Checking Progress

1. Tell the time.

_____ o'clock   half-past _____ o'clock

2. Circle the odd numbers.

5   7   12   16   19   24   27   28   33

3. How much money is this?

Ⓝ Ⓝ Ⓝ Ⓝ Ⓝ Ⓝ Ⓝ Ⓟ Ⓟ Ⓟ Ⓟ Ⓟ Ⓟ _____¢

Show the same amount using fewer coins.
Use Ⓟ, Ⓝ, and Ⓓ.

How much money is this?

Ⓓ Ⓓ Ⓝ Ⓝ Ⓝ Ⓟ Ⓟ Ⓟ _____¢

Ⓟ Ⓓ Ⓟ Ⓝ Ⓝ Ⓟ Ⓓ Ⓝ Ⓝ Ⓓ _____¢

Use with Lesson 3.15.   **305**

4. Complete the diagrams.

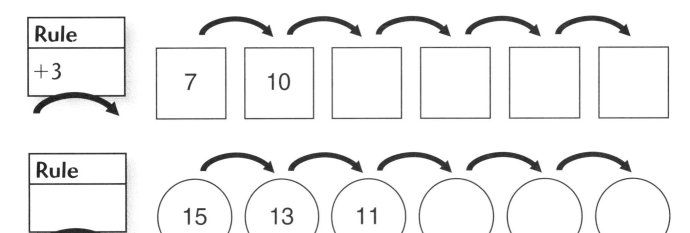

Rule
+3

7 | 10 | | | |

Rule

15 | 13 | 11 | | |

---

5. Use your number grid to help you solve these problems.

Start at 25. Count up 3 steps. You end up on _____.

$25 + 3 =$ _____

Start at 32. Count back 9 steps. You end up on _____.

$32 - 9 =$ _____

$39 + 7 =$ _____ $42 - 5 =$ _____

$45 + 10 =$ _____ $53 - 10 =$ _____

Unit 4 Checking Progress

Tell the time.

1.

half-past

_____ o'clock

2.

quarter-before

_____ o'clock

Measure to the nearest inch.

3. ——————————— _____ inches

4. ————————————— _____ inches

5. ——————————————————

_____ inches

6. Draw a line segment that is about 4 inches long.

Unit 4 Checking Progress (cont.)

7. How much money has Dolores saved?

ⒹⒹⓃⓃⓃⓃⓅⓅⓅⓅⓅ _____ ¢

Show the same amount using fewer coins.
Use Ⓟ, Ⓝ, and Ⓓ.

Write each sum.

8.

$3 + 5 =$ _____

9.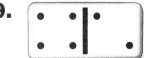

$4 + 2 =$ _____

10.

_____ $= 4 + 3$

11.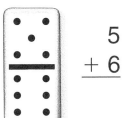

$\begin{array}{r} 5 \\ + 6 \\ \hline \end{array}$

12.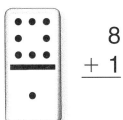

$\begin{array}{r} 8 \\ + 1 \\ \hline \end{array}$

13.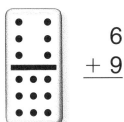

$\begin{array}{r} 6 \\ + 9 \\ \hline \end{array}$

Use with Lesson 4.13.

Unit 5 Checking Progress

Add.

1.

$3 + 3 =$ _____

2.

_____ $= 8 + 0$

3.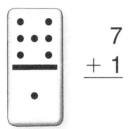

$\begin{array}{r} 7 \\ + 1 \\ \hline \end{array}$

4.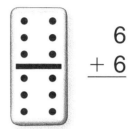

$\begin{array}{r} 6 \\ + 6 \\ \hline \end{array}$

Fill in missing dots and numbers.

5.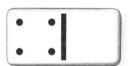

$4 +$ _____ $= 6$

6.

_____ $+ 1 = 10$

7.

$5 +$ _____ $= 10$

8.

_7_ $+$ _7_ $=$ _____

Write the number.

9.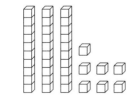

_____

10.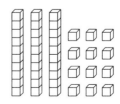

_____

Unit 5 Checking Progress (cont.)

Write <, >, or =.

11. 17 ___ 24   **12.** 32 ___ 23   **13.** 84 ___ 44   **14.** 51 ___ 56

---

15. Tina ⓟⓟⓟⓟⓟⓟⓟⓟⓟⓟ

Elise ⓟⓟⓟⓟⓟⓟⓟ

Who has more? _____   How much more? ___¢

Jerry | 26 pennies

Chris | 43 pennies

Who has more? _____   How much more? ___¢

---

16. What comes out?

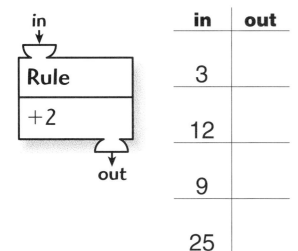

in	out
3	
12	
9	
25	

17. Find the rule. Fill in the missing numbers.

in
↓
| Rule | |
| | |
out

in	out
4	14
50	60
22	32
55	
	90

Use with Lesson 5.14.

Unit 6 Checking Progress

Tell the time.

1.

_____ : _____

2.

4:45

Measure to the nearest centimeter.

3. ——————————————————— about _____ cm

4. ————————— about _____ cm

5. $7 + 0 =$ _____ **6.** $1 + 9 =$ _____ **7.** _____ $= 4 + 4$

8.   8
   + 3

9.   6
   + 6

10.   4
   + 5

11. How much money?

Ⓓ Ⓟ Ⓟ Ⓓ Ⓓ Ⓝ
Ⓓ Ⓝ Ⓝ Ⓝ Ⓟ

_____ ¢ or $____.____

On the back of this page, show this amount with fewer coins. Use Ⓟ, Ⓝ, Ⓓ, and Ⓠ.

12. Write five names for 12.

12

Unit 7 Checking Progress

1. Circle each polygon.

---

2. Which block comes next?

Fill in the oval next to it.

0   0   0   0

---

3. Which picture is symmetrical?
Fill in the oval next to it.

0    0    0   0

Use with Lesson 7.8.

Unit 7 Checking Progress (cont.)

4. Circle the cylinder.
   Put an X through the pyramid.

  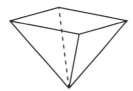

5. Complete the Fact Triangle.
   Then write the fact family.

_____

_____

_____

_____

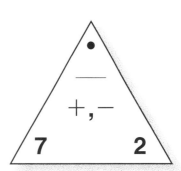

Use with Lesson 7.8.   **313**

Unit 8 Checking Progress

1. Mark the coins you need to buy a toy dinosaur.

74¢

If you pay for the dinosaur with 8 dimes,
how much change would you get back? _____

2. Draw bills and coins to show the amount you need
to buy the book.

MYSTERY

$0.10

Fill in the missing numbers.

3. 3 + ___ = 10   **4.** 14 = 7 + ___   **5.** 1 + ___ = 9

Use with Lesson 8.10.

Unit 8 Checking Progress (cont.)

Write the number shown by the base-10 blocks.

6.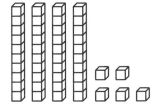

_____

7.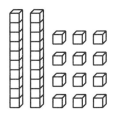

_____

8.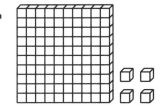

_____

Shade the fractional part of the figure.

9.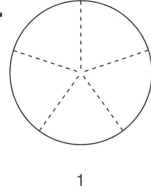

$\frac{1}{5}$

10.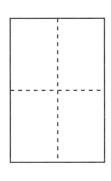

$\frac{1}{4}$

11.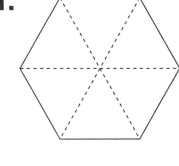

$\frac{3}{6}$

12. Three people share 12 pennies equally. Circle each person's share. Use your tool-kit coins.

How many pennies does each person get? _____

Unit 9 Checking Progress

Complete the number-grid puzzles below.

1.

| 28 |

2.

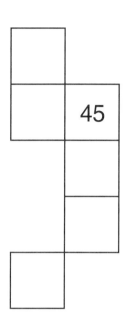

| 45 |

3.

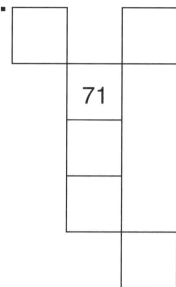

| 71 |

4. 35 + 10 = _____

5. 27 − 20 = _____

6. How much do the raccoon and the koala weigh together?

_____ pounds

23 lb   19 lb

7. How much longer is the cheetah than the rabbit?

_____ inches

57 in.   11 in.

Use with Lesson 9.9.

Unit 9 Checking Progress (cont.)

Use your template to divide the hexagons.

8. Halves

Shade $\frac{1}{2}$ of the hexagon.

9. Thirds

Shade $\frac{2}{3}$ of the hexagon.

10. Sixths

Shade $\frac{5}{6}$ of the hexagon.

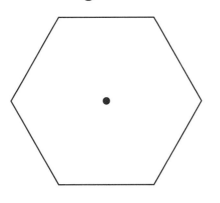
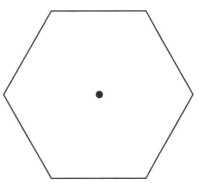
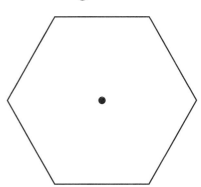

Write $>$, $<$, or $=$.

Hint: Use Problems 8–10 to help you.

| $<$ is less than |
| $>$ is greater than |
| $=$ is equal to |

11. $\frac{1}{2}$ _____ $\frac{2}{3}$

12. $\frac{1}{2}$ _____ $\frac{1}{3}$

13. $\frac{1}{3}$ _____ $\frac{5}{6}$

14. $\frac{2}{3}$ _____ $\frac{4}{6}$

15. $\frac{3}{6}$ _____ $\frac{1}{2}$

16. $\frac{5}{6}$ _____ $\frac{2}{3}$

Midyear Assessment

1. Make a tally for each number below.

28 _____

36 _____

2. Complete the table.

Before	Number	After
14	15	16
	20	
	41	
	79	
	101	

3. Fill in the frames.

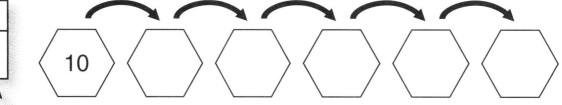

Rule
+2

Midyear Assessment (cont.)

4. Fill in the frames.

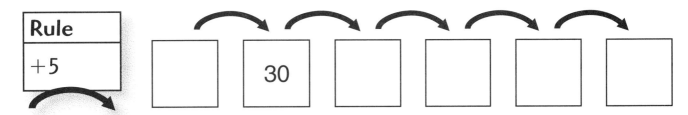

Rule
+5

30

5. Find the rule. Fill in the frames.

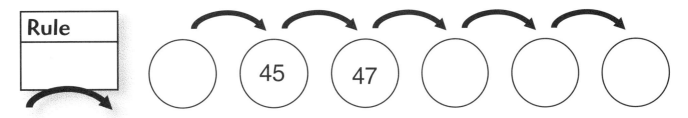

Rule

45

47

6. Draw the hands.

5 o'clock

half-past
3 o'clock

half-past
11 o'clock

Use with Lesson 5.14.

7. Write the missing numbers.

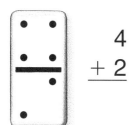

$$\begin{array}{r} 4 \\ +\ 2 \\ \hline \end{array}$$

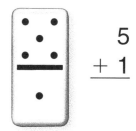

$$\begin{array}{r} 2 \\ +\ 2 \\ \hline \end{array}$$

$$\begin{array}{r} 5 \\ +\ 1 \\ \hline \end{array}$$

$3 + 3 = $ _____   _____ $= 1 + 6$ _____ $= 2 + 8$

8. Ⓓ Ⓓ Ⓝ Ⓝ Ⓝ Ⓝ Ⓝ Ⓟ Ⓟ Ⓟ

How much money is this? _____ ¢

Show the same amount using fewer coins.

9. Ⓟ Ⓓ Ⓝ Ⓝ Ⓟ Ⓟ Ⓟ Ⓓ Ⓟ Ⓝ

How much money is this? _____ ¢, or $ ___ . ___

Show the same amount using fewer coins.

Use with Lesson 5.14.

End-of-Year Assessment

1. Draw the hands.

4:00   10:30   quarter to
                                                3 o'clock

2. Tell the time.

_____:_____   _____:_____   _____:_____

3. How much money is this?

Tia _____¢ or $_____._____

Philip _____¢ or $_____._____

Who has more? _____

How much more? _____¢ or $_____._____

End-of-Year Assessment (cont.)

4. Use Ⓟ, Ⓝ, Ⓓ, and Ⓠ to show the coins you need to buy the crayons.

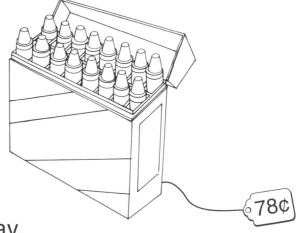

78¢

Show this amount another way.

5. Fill in the circle next to the name of each shape.

 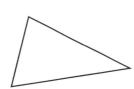 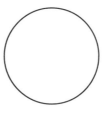 

O circle   O circle   O circle   O circle

O square   O triangle   O rectangle   O sphere

O triangle   O hexagon   O square   O cone

O rectangle   O square   O triangle   O triangle

Use with Lesson 10.7.

End-of-Year Assessment (cont.)

6. Fill in the missing numbers.

6 + ＿＿ = 8   10 = 5 + ＿＿

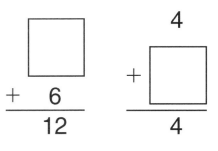

7. Complete the fact triangle and write the fact family.

＿＿ + ＿＿ = ＿＿

＿＿ + ＿＿ = ＿＿

＿＿ − ＿＿ = ＿＿

＿＿ − ＿＿ = ＿＿

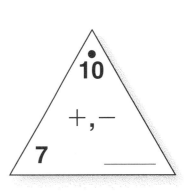

8. Fill in the missing numbers.

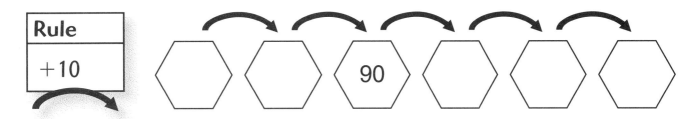

9. Find the rule. Fill in the missing numbers.

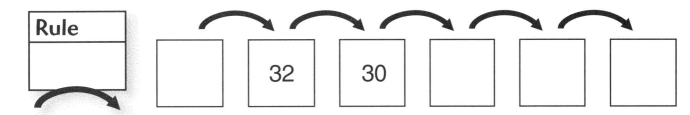

End-of-Year Assessment (cont.)

10. Find the rule and complete the table.

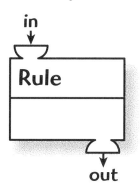

in	out
8	5
23	20
	27
	52

11. Write 6 names for 30.

30

12. Measure the line segment to the nearest inch.

_____   about _____ inches

Draw a line segment that is about 2 inches longer.

How long is this line segment?   about _____ inches

13. Measure each line segment to the nearest half-inch.

_____   about _____ inches

_____   about _____ inches

End-of-Year Assessment (cont.)

14. Measure each line segment to the nearest centimeter.

_____ about _____ cm

_____ about _____ cm

15. Solve the following problems. You may use your number grid.

18 + 5 = _____   _____ = 24 + 7   _____ = 31 − 3

$$\begin{array}{r} 38 \\ -\ 2 \\ \hline \end{array}$$
$$\begin{array}{r} 67 \\ +20 \\ \hline \end{array}$$
$$\begin{array}{r} 26 \\ -15 \\ \hline \end{array}$$

16. Use >, <, or =.

42 _____ 24

23 _____ 10 + 10

81 _____ 29

4 + 6 _____ 7 + 3

57 _____ 107

$0.32 _____ Ⓓ Ⓓ Ⓝ Ⓓ

17. Complete the number grid puzzle.

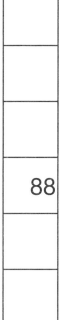

18. How much more does the raccoon weigh than
the rabbit?

raccoon

23 lb

rabbit

6 lb

about _____ pounds

19. Write the numbers shown by base-10 blocks. Circle
the right word to tell if the number is odd or even.

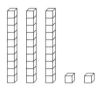   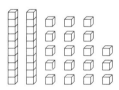   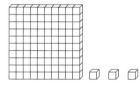

_____   _____   _____

odd or even   odd or even   odd or even

20. Write these numbers.

3 tens 5 ones   17 ones 8 tens   4 hundreds 2 tens

_____   _____   _____

End-of-Year Assessment (cont.)

21. Shade the fraction for each shape.

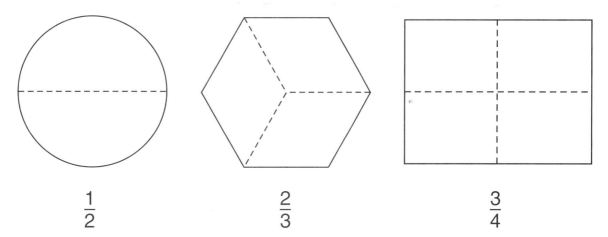

$\frac{1}{2}$ $\frac{2}{3}$ $\frac{3}{4}$

22. Terry's favorite flavor is strawberry. Add Terry's favorite flavor to the graph.

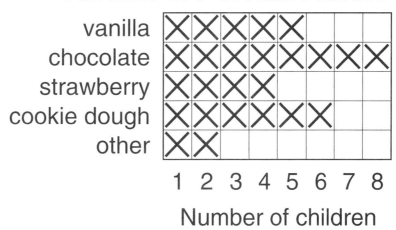

Answer the questions.

Which flavor is the most popular? _____

How many people like strawberry (counting Terry)? _____

Class Checklist: Unit 1

Class _____

Dates _____

Learning Goals

Children's Names	1a Count by 5s to 40.	1b Count by 2s to 40.	1c Write numbers from 1 to 20	1d Compare pairs of numbers less than 16.	1e Write and count tallies.	1f Count up and back by 1s, to and including 20.	1g Count 20 or more objects.					
1.												
2.												
3.												
4.												
5.												
6.												
7.												
8.												
9.												
10.												
11.												
12.												
13.												
14.												
15.												
16.												
17.												
18.												
19.												
20.												
21.												
22.												
23.												
24.												
25.												
26.												
27.												
28.												
29.												
30.												

Use with Lesson 1.14.

Individual Profile of Progress: Unit 1

Check ✔			Learning Goals	Comments
B	**D**	**S**		
			1a Count by 5s to 40.	
			1b Count by 2s to 40.	
			1c Write numbers from 1 to 20.	
			1d Compare pairs of numbers less than 16.	
			1e Write and count tallies.	
			1f Count up and back by 1s, starting with any number up to and including 20.	
			1g Count 20 or more objects.	

Notes to Parents

_____

_____

_____

_____

B = **B**eginning; **D** = **D**eveloping; **S** = **S**ecure

Class Checklist: Unit 2

Class _____

Dates _____

Learning Goals

Children's Names	2a Calculate the values of combinations of pennies and nickels.	2b Find complements of 10.	2c Solve addition and subtraction number stories.	2d Count up and back by 1s on the number grid.	2e Tell time to the nearest hour.	2f Exchange pennies for nickels.	2g Count by 2s to 40. Count by 5s to 50.					
1.												
2.												
3.												
4.												
5.												
6.												
7.												
8.												
9.												
10.												
11.												
12.												
13.												
14.												
15.												
16.												
17.												
18.												
19.												
20.												
21.												
22.												
23.												
24.												
25.												
26.												
27.												
28.												
29.												
30.												

Use with Lesson 2.14.

Child's Name   Date

Individual Profile of Progress: Unit 2

Check ✔			Learning Goals	Comments
B	**D**	**S**		
			2a Calculate the values of combinations of pennies and nickels.	
			2b Find complements of 10.	
			2c Solve addition and subtraction number stories.	
			2d Count up and back by 1s on the number grid.	
			2e Tell time to the nearest hour.	
			2f Exchange pennies for nickels.	
			2g Count by 2s to 40. Count by 5s to 50.	

Notes to Parents

_____

_____

_____

_____

B = **B**eginning; **D** = **D**eveloping; **S** = **S**ecure

Class _____

Dates _____

Learning Goals

3a Complete Frames-and-Arrows diagrams.

3b Identify and complete patterns.

3c Solve addition and subtraction problems by skip counting on the number line and the number grid.

3d Identify numbers as even or odd.

3e Know the values of pennies, nickels, and dimes, and calculate the values of combinations of these coins.

3f Tell time to the nearest half-hour.

3g Solve addition and subtraction number stories.

Children's Names	3a	3b	3c	3d	3e	3f	3g						
1.													
2.													
3.													
4.													
5.													
6.													
7.													
8.													
9.													
10.													
11.													
12.													
13.													
14.													
15.													
16.													
17.													
18.													
19.													
20.													
21.													
22.													
23.													
24.													
25.													
26.													
27.													
28.													
29.													
30.													

Individual Profile of Progress: Unit 3

Check ✔					
B	**D**	**S**	**Learning Goals**		**Comments**
			3a	Complete Frames-and-Arrows diagrams.	
			3b	Identify and complete patterns.	
			3c	Solve addition and subtraction problems by skip counting on the number line and the number grid.	
			3d	Identify numbers as even or odd.	
			3e	Know the values of pennies, nickels, and dimes, and calculate the values of combinations of these coins.	
			3f	Tell time to the nearest half-hour.	
			3g	Solve addition and subtraction number stories.	

Notes to Parents

_____

_____

_____

_____

B = **B**eginning; **D** = **D**eveloping; **S** = **S**ecure

Use with Lesson 3.15.

Class _____

Dates _____

Learning Goals

4a Use standard units for measuring length.

4b Find sums and missing addends.

4c Calculate the values of combinations of pennies, nickels, and dimes.

4d Solve addition and subtraction number stories.

4e Order and compare numbers to 22.

4f Tell time to the nearest half-hour.

Children's Names	4a	4b	4c	4d	4e	4f							
1.													
2.													
3.													
4.													
5.													
6.													
7.													
8.													
9.													
10.													
11.													
12.													
13.													
14.													
15.													
16.													
17.													
18.													
19.													
20.													
21.													
22.													
23.													
24.													
25.													
26.													
27.													
28.													
29.													
30.													

Individual Profile of Progress: Unit 4

Check ✔				
B	**D**	**S**	**Learning Goals**	**Comments**
			4a Use standard units for measuring length.	
			4b Find sums and missing addends.	
			4c Calculate the values of combinations of pennies, nickels, and dimes.	
			4d Solve addition and subtraction number stories.	
			4e Order and compare numbers to 22.	
			4f Tell time to the nearest half-hour.	

Notes to Parents

_____

_____

_____

_____

B = **B**eginning; **D** = **D**eveloping; **S** = **S**ecure

Class Checklist: Unit 5

Class _____

Dates _____

Learning Goals

Children's Names	5a Find missing numbers and/or the missing rule in "What's My Rule?" problems.	5b Understand place value for tens and ones.	5c Compare numbers using < and >.	5d Know +1, +0, doubles, and sums of 10 addition facts.	5e Solve addition and subtraction number stories.								
1.													
2.													
3.													
4.													
5.													
6.													
7.													
8.													
9.													
10.													
11.													
12.													
13.													
14.													
15.													
16.													
17.													
18.													
19.													
20.													
21.													
22.													
23.													
24.													
25.													
26.													
27.													
28.													
29.													
30.													

Use with Lesson 5.14.

Individual Profile of Progress: Unit 5

Check ✔				
B	**D**	**S**	**Learning Goals**	**Comments**
			5a Find missing numbers and/or the missing rule in "What's My Rule?" problems.	
			5b Understand place value for tens and ones.	
			5c Compare numbers using < and >.	
			5d Know +1, +0, doubles, and sums of 10 addition facts.	
			5e Solve addition and subtraction number stories.	

Notes to Parents

_____

_____

_____

_____

B = **B**eginning; **D** = **D**eveloping; **S** = **S**ecure

Class _____

Dates _____

Learning Goals

- **6a** Measure objects to the nearest centimeter.
- **6b** Understand digital notation for time.
- **6c** Know addition facts.
- **6d** Calculate the value of combinations of pennies, nickels, dimes, and quarters.
- **6e** Find equivalent names for a number.

Children's Names

	6a	6b	6c	6d	6e						
1.											
2.											
3.											
4.											
5.											
6.											
7.											
8.											
9.											
10.											
11.											
12.											
13.											
14.											
15.											
16.											
17.											
18.											
19.											
20.											
21.											
22.											
23.											
24.											
25.											
26.											
27.											
28.											
29.											
30.											

Use with Lesson 6.13.

Individual Profile of Progress: Unit 6

Check ✔			Learning Goals	Comments
B	**D**	**S**		
			6a Measure objects to the nearest centimeter.	
			6b Understand digital notation for time.	
			6c Learn simple addition facts.	
			6d Calculate the value of coin combinations: P, N, D, and Q.	
			6e Find many names for a number.	

Notes to Parents

_____

_____

_____

_____

B = **B**eginning; **D** = **D**eveloping; **S** = **S**ecure

Class Checklist: Unit 7

Class _____

Dates _____

Learning Goals

7a Identify 3-dimensional shapes and know their characteristics.

7b Identify symmetrical figures.

7c Sort and identify objects by attributes.

7d Identify polygons and know their characteristics.

7e Know addition facts.

Children's Names	7a	7b	7c	7d	7e							
1.												
2.												
3.												
4.												
5.												
6.												
7.												
8.												
9.												
10.												
11.												
12.												
13.												
14.												
15.												
16.												
17.												
18.												
19.												
20.												
21.												
22.												
23.												
24.												
25.												
26.												
27.												
28.												
29.												
30.												

Use with Lesson 7.8.

Individual Profile of Progress: Unit 7

Check ✔				
B	**D**	**S**	**Learning Goals**	**Comments**
			7a Identify 3-dimensional shapes and know their characteristics.	
			7b Identify symmetrical figures.	
			7c Sort and identify objects by attributes.	
			7d Identify polygons and know their characteristics.	
			7e Know addition facts.	

Notes to Parents

_____

_____

_____

_____

B = **B**eginning; **D** = **D**eveloping; **S** = **S**ecure

Class Checklist: Unit 8

Class _____

Dates _____

Learning Goals

- **8a** Make change for amounts less than $1.
- **8b** Identify fractional parts of regions and sets with a focus on unit fractions.
- **8c** Calculate the values of combinations of pennies, nickels, dimes, and quarters.
- **8d** Solve addition and subtraction number stories.
- **8e** Understand place value for tens and ones.
- **8f** Know addition facts.

Children's Names	8a	8b	8c	8d	8e	8f						
1.												
2.												
3.												
4.												
5.												
6.												
7.												
8.												
9.												
10.												
11.												
12.												
13.												
14.												
15.												
16.												
17.												
18.												
19.												
20.												
21.												
22.												
23.												
24.												
25.												
26.												
27.												
28.												
29.												
30.												

Use with Lesson 8.10.

Individual Profile of Progress: Unit 8

Check ✔				
B	**D**	**S**	**Learning Goals**	**Comments**
			8a Make change for amounts less than $1.	
			8b Identify fractional parts of regions and sets with a focus on unit fractions.	
			8c Calculate the values of combinations of pennies, nickels, dimes, and quarters.	
			8d Solve addition and subtraction number stories.	
			8e Understand place value for tens and ones.	
			8f Know addition facts.	

Notes to Parents

_____

_____

_____

_____

B = **B**eginning; **D** = **D**eveloping; **S** = **S**ecure

Class Checklist: Unit 9

Class _____

Dates _____

Children's Names	Learning Goals	9a Solve 2-digit addition and subtraction problems.	9b Compare fractions less than 1.	9c Find equivalent fractions for given fractions.	9d Identify fractional parts of a region.	9e Identify and use patterns on the number grid						
1.												
2.												
3.												
4.												
5.												
6.												
7.												
8.												
9.												
10.												
11.												
12.												
13.												
14.												
15.												
16.												
17.												
18.												
19.												
20.												
21.												
22.												
23.												
24.												
25.												
26.												
27.												
28.												
29.												
30.												

Individual Profile of Progress: Unit 9

Check ✔				
B	**D**	**S**	**Learning Goals**	**Comments**
			9a Solve 2-digit addition and subtraction problems.	
			9b Compare fractions less than 1.	
			9c Find equivalent fractions for given fractions.	
			9d Identify fractional parts of a region.	
			9e Identify and use patterns on the number grid.	

Notes to Parents

_____

_____

_____

_____

B = **B**eginning; **D** = **D**eveloping; **S** = **S**ecure

Class _____

Dates _____

Learning Goals

1. Count by 5s to 40. **(1a)**
2. Count by 2s to 40. **(1b)**
3. Count by 2s to 40. Count by 5s to 50. **(2g)**
4. Count up and back by 1s, starting with any number up to and including 20. **(1f)**
5. Count up and back by 1s on the number grid. **(2d)**
6. Count 20 or more objects. **(1g)**
7. Write numbers from 1 to 20. **(1c)**
8. Write and count tallies. **(1e)**
9. Compare pairs of numbers. **(1d)**
10. Find complements of 10. **(2b)**
11. Solve addition and subtraction number stories. **(2c)**
12. Calculate the values of combinations of pennies and nickels. **(2a)**
13. Exchange pennies for nickels. **(2f)**
14. Tell time to the nearest hour. **(2e)**

Children's Names	1.	2.	3.	4.	5.	6.	7.	8.	9.	10.	11.	12.	13.	14.
1.														
2.														
3.														
4.														
5.														
6.														
7.														
8.														
9.														
10.														
11.														
12.														
13.														
14.														
15.														
16.														
17.														
18.														
19.														
20.														
21.														
22.														
23.														
24.														
25.														
26.														
27.														
28.														
29.														
30.														

Use with Lesson 2.14.

Individual Profile of Progress: 1st Quarter

Check ✔				
B	**D**	**S**	**Learning Goals**	**Comments**
			1. Count by 5s to 40. **(1a)**	
			2. Count by 2s to 40. **(1b)**	
			3. Count by 2s to 40. Count by 5s to 50. **(2g)**	
			4. Count up and back by 1s, starting with any number up to and including 20. **(1f)**	
			5. Count up and back by 1s on the number grid. **(2d)**	
			6. Count 20 or more objects. **(1g)**	
			7. Write numbers from 1 to 20. **(1c)**	
			8. Write and count tallies. **(1e)**	
			9. Compare pairs of numbers less than 16. **(1d)**	
			10. Find complements of 10. **(2b)**	
			11. Solve addition and subtraction number stories. **(2c)**	
			12. Calculate the values of combinations of pennies and nickels. **(2a)**	
			13. Exchange pennies for nickels. **(2f)**	
			14. Tell time to the nearest hour. **(2e)**	

Notes to Parents

_____

_____

_____

_____

B = Beginning; D = Developing; S = Secure

Class Checklist: 2nd Quarter

Class _____

Dates _____

Learning Goals

1. Complete Frames-and-Arrows diagrams. **(3a)**
2. Identify and complete patterns. **(3b)**
3. Solve addition and Subtraction problems by skip counting on the number line and the number grid. **(3c)**
4. Find sums and missing addends. **(4b)**
5. Know + 1, + 0, doubles, and sums of 10 addition facts. **(5d)**
6. Find missing numbers and/or sums of "What's My Rule?" problems. **(5a)**
7. Identify numbers and/or the missing rule in problems. **(5a)**
8. Identify numbers as even or odd. **(3d)**
9. Order and compare numbers to 22. **(4e)**
10. Compare numbers using < and >. **(5c)**
11. Understand place value for tens and ones. **(5b)**
12. Solve addition and subtraction number stories. **(3g, 4d, 5e)**
13. Know the values of pennies, nickels, and dimes, and calculate the values of combinations of these coins. **(3e, 4c)**
14. Use standard units for measuring length. **(4a)**
15. Tell time to the nearest half-hour. **(3f, 4f)**

Children's Names	1.	2.	3.	4.	5.	6.	7.	8.	9.	10.	11.	12.	13.	14.
1.														
2.														
3.														
4.														
5.														
6.														
7.														
8.														
9.														
10.														
11.														
12.														
13.														
14.														
15.														
16.														
17.														
18.														
19.														
20.														
21.														
22.														
23.														
24.														
25.														
26.														
27.														
28.														
29.														
30.														

Use with Lesson 5.14.

Individual Profile of Progress: 2nd Quarter

Check ✔			Learning Goals	Comments
B	**D**	**S**		
			1. Complete Frames-and-Arrows diagrams. **(3a)**	
			2. Identify and complete patterns. **(3b)**	
			3. Solve addition and subtraction problems by skip counting on the number line and the number grid. **(3c)**	
			4. Find sums and missing addends. **(4b)**	
			5. Know +1, +0, doubles, and sums of 10 addition facts. **(5d)**	
			6. Find missing numbers and/or the missing rule in "What's My Rule?" problems. **(5a)**	
			7. Identify numbers as even or odd. **(3d)**	
			8. Order and compare numbers to 22. **(4e)**	
			9. Compare numbers using < and >. **(5c)**	
			10. Understand place value for tens and ones. **(5b)**	
			11. Solve addition and subtraction number stories. **(3g, 4d, 5e)**	
			12. Know the values of pennies, nickels, and dimes, and calculate the values of combinations of these coins. **(3e, 4c)**	
			13. Use standard units for measuring length. **(4a)**	
			14. Tell time to the nearest half-hour. **(3f, 4f)**	

Notes to Parents

_____

_____

_____

B = **B**eginning; D = **D**eveloping; S = **S**ecure

Class _____

Dates _____

Learning Goals

1. Measure objects to the nearest centimeter. **(6a)**
2. Understand digital notation for time. **(6b)**
3. Calculate the values of combinations of pennies, nickels, dimes, and quarters. **(6d, 8c)**
4. Make change for amounts less than $1. **(8a)**
5. Understand place value for tens and ones. **(8e)**
6. Find equivalent names for a number. **(6e)**
7. Identify 3-dimensional shapes and know their characteristics. **(7a)**
8. Identify symmetrical figures. **(7b)**
9. Sort and identify objects by attributes. **(7d)**
10. Identify polygons and know their characteristics. **(7c)**
11. Identify fractional parts of regions and sets with a focus on unit fractions. **(8b)**
12. Know addition facts. **(6c, 7e, 8f)**
13. Solve addition and subtraction number stories. **(8d)**

Children's Names

	1	2	3	4	5	6	7	8	9	10	11	12	13		
1.															
2.															
3.															
4.															
5.															
6.															
7.															
8.															
9.															
10.															
11.															
12.															
13.															
14.															
15.															
16.															
17.															
18.															
19.															
20.															
21.															
22.															
23.															
24.															
25.															
26.															
27.															
28.															
29.															
30.															

Use with Lesson 8.10.

Individual Profile of Progress: 3rd Quarter

Check ✔			Learning Goals	Comments
B	**D**	**S**		
			1. Measure objects to the nearest centimeter. **(6a)**	
			2. Understand digital notation for time. **(6b)**	
			3. Calculate the values of combinations of pennies, nickels, dimes, and quarters. **(6d, 8c)**	
			4. Make change for amounts less than $1. **(8a)**	
			5. Understand place value for tens and ones. **(8e)**	
			6. Find equivalent names for a number. **(6e)**	
			7. Identify 3-dimensional shapes and know their characteristics. **(7a)**	
			8. Identify symmetrical figures. **(7b)**	
			9. Sort and identify objects by attributes. **(7c)**	
			10. Identify polygons and know their characteristics. **(7d)**	
			11. Identify fractional parts of regions and sets with a focus on unit fractions. **(8b)**	
			12. Know addition facts. **(6c, 7e, 8f)**	
			13. Solve addition and subtraction number stories. **(8d)**	

Notes to Parents

_____

_____

_____

B = **B**eginning; **D** = **D**eveloping; **S** = **S**ecure

Class Checklist: 4th Quarter

Class _____

Dates _____

Learning Goals

1. Solve 2-digit addition and subtraction problems. (9a)
2. Identify and use patterns on the number grid. (9e)
3. Compare fractions less than 1. (9b)
4. Find equivalent fractions for given fractions. (9c)
5. Identify fractional parts of a region. (9d)

Children's Names	1.	2.	3.	4.	5.								
1.													
2.													
3.													
4.													
5.													
6.													
7.													
8.													
9.													
10.													
11.													
12.													
13.													
14.													
15.													
16.													
17.													
18.													
19.													
20.													
21.													
22.													
23.													
24.													
25.													
26.													
27.													
28.													
29.													
30.													

Use with Lesson 10.7.

Child's Name   Date

Individual Profile of Progress: 4th Quarter ✔

B	D	S	Learning Goals	Comments
			Check ✔	
			1. Solve 2-digit addition and subtraction problems. **(9a)**	
			2. Identify and use patterns on the number grid. **(9e)**	
			3. Compare fractions less than 1. **(9b)**	
			4. Find equivalent fractions for given fractions. **(9c)**	
			5. Identify fractional parts of a region. **(9d)**	

Notes to Parents

_____

_____

_____

_____

B = **B**eginning; **D** = **D**eveloping; **S** = **S**ecure

Use with Lesson 10.7.

List of Assessment Sources

Ongoing Assessment

_____

_____

_____

_____

Product Assessment

_____

_____

_____

_____

Periodic Assessment

_____

_____

_____

_____

Outside Tests

_____

_____

_____

_____

Other

_____

_____

_____

_____

Use as needed.

Individual Profile of Progress

Check ✔				
B	**D**	**S**	**Learning Goals**	**Comments**
			1.	
			2.	
			3.	
			4.	
			5.	
			6.	
			7.	
			8.	
			9.	
			10.	

Notes to Parents

_____

_____

_____

_____

_____

_____

_____

B = **B**eginning; **D** = **D**eveloping; **S** = **S**ecure

Use as needed.

Class Checklist

Class _____

Dates _____

Learning Goals

Children's Names

1.														
2.														
3.														
4.														
5.														
6.														
7.														
8.														
9.														
10.														
11.														
12.														
13.														
14.														
15.														
16.														
17.														
18.														
19.														
20.														
21.														
22.														
23.														
24.														
25.														
26.														
27.														
28.														
29.														
30.														

Use as needed.

1.		1.		1.	
2.		2.		2.	
3.		3.		3.	
4.		4.		4.	
5.		5.		5.	
6.		6.		6.	
7.		7.		7.	
8.		8.		8.	
9.		9.		9.	
10.		10.		10.	
11.		11.		11.	
12.		12.		12.	
13.		13.		13.	
14.		14.		14.	
15.		15.		15.	
16.		16.		16.	
17.		17.		17.	
18.		18.		18.	
19.		19.		19.	
20.		20.		20.	
21.		21.		21.	
22.		22.		22.	
23.		23.		23.	
24.		24.		24.	
25.		25.		25.	
26.		26.		26.	
27.		27.		27.	
28.		28.		28.	
29.		29.		29.	
30.		30.		30.	

Use as needed.

Class Progress Indicator

Mathematical Topic Being Assessed: _____

	BEGINNING	DEVELOPING OR DEVELOPING+	SECURE OR SECURE+
First Assessment After Lesson: _____ Dates included: _____ to _____			
Second Assessment After Lesson: _____ Dates included: _____ to _____			
Third Assessment After Lesson: _____ Dates included: _____ to _____			

Notes

_____

_____

_____

_____

Use as needed.

Parent Reflections

Use some of the following questions (or your own) and tell us how you see your child progressing in mathematics.

Do you see evidence of your child using mathematics at home?

What do you think are your child's strengths and challenges in mathematics?

Does your child demonstrate responsibility for completing Home Links?

What thoughts do you have about your child's progress in mathematics?

Rubric

Beginning (B)

Developing (D)

Secure (S)

Use as needed.

About My Math Class

Draw a face or write the words that show how you feel.

Good   OK   Not so good

1. This is how I feel about math.	**2.** This is how I feel about working with others.	**3.** This is how I feel about working by myself.
4. This is how I feel about number stories.	**5.** This is how I feel about doing Home Links.	**6.** This is how I feel about solving problems.

Circle **yes, sometimes,** or **no.**

7. I like to figure things out. I am curious.

yes   sometimes no

8. I keep trying even when I don't understand something right away.

yes   sometimes no

Name

Date

Math Log A

What did you learn in mathematics this week?

Use as needed.

Math Log B

Question:

Math Log C

Work Box

Tell how you solved
this problem.

_____

_____

_____

_____

Use as needed.

Math Log C

Work Box

Tell how you solved
this problem.

_____

_____

_____

_____

Use as needed.

Name _____   Date _____

Good Work!

☺ I like this work because

_____

- -

_____

_____

- -

_____

_____

- -

_____

_____

- -

_____

_____

- -

_____

_____

- -

_____

Use as needed.

My Work

This work shows that I can _____

_____

_____.

I am still learning to _____

_____

_____.

Use as needed.

My Work

This is what I know about _____

_____

_____

_____

Use as needed.

Name _____   Date _____

My Exit Slip

Use as needed.

- -

Name _____   Date _____

My Exit Slip

Use as needed.

A Number Story

_____

_____

_____

_____

_____

_____

_____

_____

Use as needed.

"What's My Rule?"

1. What's My Rule?

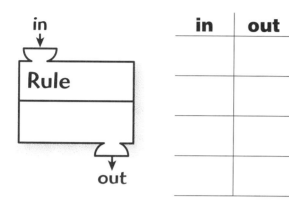

in	out

2. What's My Rule?

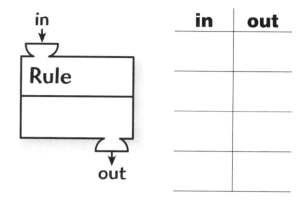

in	out

3. What's My Rule?

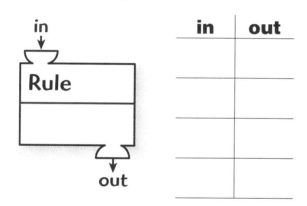

in	out

4. What's My Rule?

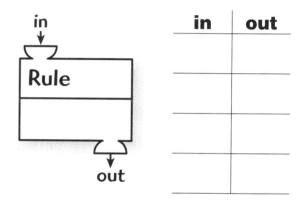

in	out

5. What's My Rule?

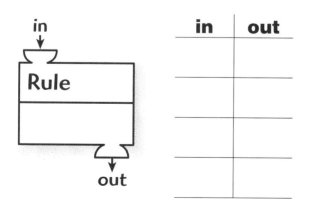

in	out

6. What's My Rule?

in	out